Building Special Operations Rela
with Fragile Partners:
Best Practices from Iraq, Syria, a....

Torsten Gojowsky
Sebastian Koegler

Building Special Operations Relationships with Fragile Partners
Best Practices from Iraq, Syria, and Afghanistan

Torsten Gojowsky
Sebastian Koegler

2019

Carola Hartmann Miles-Verlag

Bibliografische Information der Deutschen Nationalbibliothek
Die Deutsche Nationalbibliothek verzeichnet diese Publikation in der
Deutschen Nationalbibliografie; detaillierte bibliografische Daten sind
im Internet über www.dnb.de abrufbar.

© Carola Hartmann Miles-Verlag, Berlin
George-Caylay-Str. 38, 14089 Berlin
email: miles-verlag@t-online.de
www.miles-verlag.jimdo.com

Herstellung: Books on Demand GmbH, Norderstedt

Titelbild: Torsten Gojowsky, Sebastian Koegler

Printed in Germany

ISBN 978-3-945861-88-2

ABSTRACT

Relationships empower Special Operations Forces (SOF) to perform as a highly skilled and reliable cadre in collaboration with local partner forces to prevent and solve shared problem sets, often accomplishing more with less. Since 9/11, however, relationships between SOF and their partners have not always been properly built and maintained. The authors trace the causal effects of constraints, trainings, and incentives and their impact on the current North Atlantic Treaty Organization (NATO) SOF approach of building enduring relationships.

Motivated by numerous deployments to Afghanistan, Iraq, and Syria, with recurring problem sets, we chose to conduct a structured-focused comparison between U.S. and Danish SOF supporting Operation Inherent Resolve in Al Anbar, Iraq (2015–2018) and German SOF during the shift of the NATO-led International Security Assistance Force to Resolute Support mission in Afghanistan (2013–2015). The analysis of these cases finds that specific interactions of the studied factors not only cause variations in relationships between SOF and partner forces, but ultimately influence operations and objectives determining mission success or failure.

With further testing of our analysis and recommendations, this research can help to identify inherently flexible and nested strategic options for SOF senior leaders, allowing them to deploy SOF elements efficiently during times of asymmetric, diffuse, and episodic conflicts.

TABLE OF CONTENTS

LIST OF FIGURES

LIST OF ACRONYMS AND ABBREVIATIONS

AAAB	Ayn al-Asad Airbase
AAF	Afghan Air Force
AFB	A'ali al-Furat Battalion
ANDSF	Afghan Defense and Security Forces
AO	Area of Operations
ASSF	Afghan Special Security Forces
BGL	Baghlan
BLK	Balkh
BN	Battalion
BPC	Building Partner Capacity
C2	Command and Control
CAS	Close Air Support
CIA	Central Intelligence Agency
CJSOTF-I	Combined Joint Special Operations Task Force-Iraq
CJSOTF-S	Combined Joint Special Operations Task Force-Syria
COG	Center of Gravity
COIN	Counterinsurgency
COIN-FM	Counterinsurgency Field Manual
DA	Direct Action
DANSOF	Danish SOF
DoD	Department of Defense
GDPSU	General Command of Police Special Unit
GERSOF	German SOF
GFC	Ground Force Commander
GSG9	Grenzschutzgruppe 9
GWOT	Global War on Terrorism
HRO	Hostage Release Operation
ISAF	International Security Assistance Force

ISIS	Islamic State of Iraq and Syria
IW	Irregular Warfare
JP	Joint Publication
KDZ	Kunduz
KLE	Key Leader Engagement
KSK	Kommando Spezialkräfte
LOAC	Law of Armed Conflict
MA	Military Assistance
MEDEVAC	Medical Evacuation
MOI	Ministry of Interior
NATO	North Atlantic Treaty Organization
NSOCC-A	NATO Special Operations Component Command–Afghanistan
NSS	National Security Strategy
NSW	Navy Special Warfare Group
ODA	Operational Detachment-Alpha
OEF	Operation Enduring Freedom
OFS	Operation Freedom's Sentinel
OIR	Operation Inherent Resolve
OSS	Office of Strategic Services
PCOP	Provincial Chief of Police
PSU	Provincial Special Unit
ROE	Rules of Engagements
RS	Resolute Support
SFG	Special Forces Group
SFOD-G	Special Forces Operational Detachment-Golf
SMW	Special Mission Wing
SOF	Special Operations Forces
SOST	Special Operations Surgical Team
SOTF-W	Special Operations Task Force-West
SR	Special Reconnaissance
TAA	Train, Advise, and Assist

TSOC	Theater Special Operations Command
TTP	Tactics, Techniques, and Procedures
USASOC	United States Army Special Operations Command
USCENTCOM	United States Central Command
UW	Unconventional Warfare

ACKNOWLEDGMENTS

We would like to thank our advisors, Dr. Leo Blanken and Dr. Robert Burks, for their tremendous insights and recommendations throughout our research. We also would like to extend our sincere appreciation to all of our NPS professors, especially to Colonel Michael Richardson, Colonel Ian Rice, Dr. Gordon McCormick, and Dr. Kate Egerton, who shared their knowledge, experience, and wisdom during our thesis research.

In particular, I also would like to thank General (Retired) Stanley A. McChrystal, Lieutenant General (Retired) Charles Cleveland, Lieutenant General (Retired) Kenneth Tovo, Lieutenant General Michael K. Nagata, Major General Kurt Crytzer, Brigadier General Edwin J. Deedrick Jr., Brigadier General John W. Brennan, Colonel Michael G. Harris, Colonel Joseph G. Lock, Lieutenant Colonel Alvin Word IV, Lieutenant Colonel Duane Mosier, Sergeant Major (Retired) Martin Moore, and John V. Sealock for their respective support and allowing me the opportunity to further develop as a military leader.

I also would like to thank my co-author, Sebastian Koegler, for his dedication and commitment to jointly research and develop this thesis. Like in real life, teamwork and forming a NATO SOF alliance will enhance capabilities that will complement each other's efforts, enhancing strategic success. Finally, my utmost gratitude goes to my family. My wife, Caroline, who steadfastly accompanies me throughout life, and our two daughters, Vivienne and Meryem, who share their enduring love and support, which I will never forget.

—*Torsten Gojowsky*

We owe particular debt to our advisors, Dr. Leo Blanken, and Dr. Robert Burks, who gave us the academic guidance. Furthermore, the thoughtful cooperation I shared with my co-author, Torsten Gojowsky, made this thesis possible.

I especially thank my beloved wife, Antonina, and my son, Maximilian, who accompanied me with patience and indulgence.

—*Sebastian Koegler*

I. INTRODUCTION

The invasion of Afghanistan in October 2001 was the U.S.-led response to the September 11, 2001, (9/11) terrorist attacks and signified the official launch of the United States' Global War on Terrorism (GWOT).[1] The 9/11 attacks ultimately took the United States and its allies into one of their costliest and longest wars—Afghanistan.[2] The 9/11 attacks and the Afghan conflict, followed by the 2003 invasion of Iraq and the war against the Islamic State in Iraq and Syria (ISIS), brought the phenomenon of radical Islamist terrorism to the forefront of the international community's public conscience. Although the Pentagon planned the U.S. invasion of Afghanistan as a response to the terrorist attacks, it failed to determine an end state for its strategy.[3] The United States knows how to employ conventional forces against adversarial state-actors, but running Special Operations Forces (SOF) against an unconventional enemy, the non-state actors, was new to the Pentagon.[4]

The invasion of Afghanistan initially succeeded in conjunction with the Central Intelligence Agency's (CIA) plan that involved bringing together intelligence resources, sophisticated technologies, CIA paramilitary units, and leaders of the Northern Alliance, combined with U.S. military air power and Special Forces.[5] Building relationships and enabling the Northern Alliance through direct support became the cornerstone for effective, enduring collaboration. Yet, the

---

[1] "September 11th Terror Attacks Fast Facts," CNN, accessed July 27, 2013, http://www.cnn.com/2013/07/27/us/september-11-anniversary-fast-facts/index.html

[2] "Operation Iraqi Freedom and Operation New Dawn Fast Facts," CNN, October 30, 2013, http://www.cnn.com/2013/10/30/world/meast/operation-iraqi-freedom-and-operation-new-dawn-fast-facts/index.html.

[3] Hy S. Rothstein, *Afghanistan and the Troubled Future of Unconventional Warfare* (Annapolis, MD: Naval Institute Press, 2006), 12–14.

[4] David Fitzgerald, *Learning to Forget: U.S. Army Counterinsurgency Doctrine and Practice from Vietnam to Iraq* (Stanford, CA: Stanford University Press, 2013).

[5] Steve Coll, *Ghost Wars: The Secret History of the CIA, Afghanistan, and Bin Laden, from the Soviet Invasion to September 10, 2001* (New York: Penguin Books, 2004), 9–14.

command and control (C2) structures developed in more conventional ways could not adequately react when the nature of the war became unconventional.[6] The failure to capture or kill Osama bin Laden in 2001/2002 taught the Western military that partnering with Afghan forces was more successful when Western purposes dovetailed with local interests.[7] During the following years of the conflict, the bureaucratized military reproduced its own image, sacrificing established relationships to political expediency, resulting in America's longest war.[8] The fundamental lessons from the Afghan conflict, an essential example of an asymmetric war, have not been adequately addressed, leading to similar follow-on failures in Iraq and Syria.

One of the most pressing questions emerges from lessons related to the conventional U.S. strategy that proved ineffective in the Afghan conflict: what if the unique relationships of CIA specialized units with the mujahedeen and warlords fighting Soviet forces in the 1980s had been maintained to acquire situational awareness in Afghanistan throughout the rise of international terrorism in the 1990s?[9] We explore this question in this research effort.

A.   Purpose

Long-lasting North Atlantic Treaty Organization (NATO) SOF engagements in asymmetric wars were intended to build security institutions and partner capacities through mirroring Western police and military frameworks.[10] The partner forces, who have trained for years, along with Western SOF advisors, are neither winning nor losing the wars against their adaptable opponents like in Afghanistan, Iraq, and

---

[6] Hy S. Rothstein, "A Tale of Two Wars: Why the U.S. Cannot Conduct Unconventional Warfare" (PhD diss., Tufts University, MA: 2004), 134–143.

[7] Jack Fairweather, *The Good War: Why We Couldn't Win the War or the Peace in Afghanistan* (New York: Basic Books, 2014), 10–12.

[8] Peter Bergen, *The Longest War: The Enduring Conflict between America and Al-Qaeda* (New York: Free Press, 2011).

[9] Steve Coll, *Directorate S: The C.I.A. and America's Secret Wars in Afghanistan and Pakistan* (New York: Penguin Books, 2018), 5–7.

[10] Theo Farrell, Frans P. B. Osinga, and James A. Russell, eds., *Military Adaptation in Afghanistan* (Stanford, CA: Stanford University Press, 2013).

Syria.[11] Repeated failures, but also successes, in these campaigns emphasize the need to analyze how NATO SOF units build and especially maintain relationships with their partner forces in asymmetric wars.[12] Motivated by numerous deployments to Afghanistan, Iraq, and Syria with recurring problem sets, the authors use relevant literature and case studies about building enduring relationships to analyze contemporary SOF tactics, techniques, and procedures (TTP). The purpose of this study is to focus on relationships between NATO SOF and their local partners on the tactical level during conflict to identify key components of relationships and analyze their effectiveness.

The constraints on NATO SOF engaging in conflict zones determine the foundation of the possible outcomes of their SOF advisors. Constraints such as mandates, doctrines, rules of engagement (ROE), or manuals, but also the organizational and individual limitations of each SOF unit, are crucial factors for working with partner nation forces. Additionally, each nation has its own national caveats that often hamper combined SOF operations.[13] Even under the same umbrella of constraints, each nation has its own approaches and therefore different outcomes in building enduring relationships. Hence, NATO SOF needs to identify and assess how to best position and sustain units along with their partners to be more operationally effective in these types of conflicts. Therefore, the constraints and their implications for the SOF advisors require more analysis.

The training of partner forces in order to establish security structures seems to be the predominant answer to prolonged military involvements, often with questionable outcomes. The collapse of the Iraqi army facing ISIS in 2014 and the short occupation of Kunduz

---

[11] C. J. Chivers, "War without End," *New York Times,* August 8, 2018, https://www.nytimes.com/2018/08/08/magazine/war-afghanistan-iraq-soldiers.html.

[12] Anthony H. Cordesman, "U.S. Wars in Iraq, Syria, Libya and Yemen: What Are the Endstates?" CSIS, August 15, 2016, https://www.csis.org/analysis/us-wars-iraq-syria-libya-and-yemen-what-are-endstates.

[13] Spencer Tucker and Paul G. Pierpaoli, *U.S. Conflicts in the 21st Century: Afghanistan War, Iraq War, and the War on Terror* (Santa Barbara, CA: ABC-CLIO, 2016).

city by the Taliban in 2015 challenge the sustainability of yearlong-trained partner forces operating without their advisors.[14] Even after short-lived initial successes in both campaigns, SOF units soon found themselves in long-lasting counterinsurgency (COIN) fights. Certainly, the purpose and objectives of training partner forces in asymmetric wars should be reassessed.[15] This will give SOF advisors more realistic and achievable goals to enhance their operational effectiveness tailored to the partner forces, and foremost, provide the policy decision makers with the needed situational awareness to adjust the policy and strategy accordingly.[16]

Analyzing constraints and training alone may ignore another essential factor, especially in fragile or failed states with partner forces lacking national identity and loyalty: incentives. Western allies created, trained, and equipped Afghan and Iraqi security forces who were simply not willing to fight hard enough and die for the weak, corrupt, Western-backed and, foremost, illegitimate governments in Kabul and Baghdad.[17] Conversely, M. Chris Mason claims that absolutely dedicated to battlefield success, the insurgents are completely confident of the final victory of their cause, because they believe in their cause enough to die for it. The use of incentives seems to be necessary to face the motivational disparity between partner forces and their adversaries. Contemporary NATO SOF trends using various incentives during training and operations have to be taken into consideration when examining the effectiveness of building enduring relationships.

---

[14] Joseph Goldstein and Mujib Mashal, "Taliban Fighters Capture Kunduz City as Afghan Forces Retreat," *New York Times,* September 29, 2015, https://www.nytimes.com/2015/09/29/world/asia/taliban-fighters-enter-city-of-kunduz-in-northern-afghanistan.html.

[15] John Alvarez et al., *Special Operations Forces Reference Manual* (Tampa, FL: Joint Special Operations University, 2015).

[16] Todd C. Helmus, *Advising the Command: Best Practices from the Special Operation's Advisory Experience in Afghanistan* (Santa Monica, CA: RAND Corporation, 2015).

[17] M. Chris Mason, *The Strategic Lessons Unlearned from Vietnam, Iraq, and Afghanistan: Why the Afghan National Security Forces Will Not Hold, and the Implications for the U.S. Army in Afghanistan* (Carlisle, PA: Strategic Studies Institute, 2015), 137–138.

Studying these three factors—constraints, training, and incentives—and their effects on current NATO SOF approaches of building enduring relationships have been argued to be crucial for the indirect strategy in current and future conflicts.[18] This study will help to identify and provide inherently flexible and nested strategic options to SOF senior leaders, allowing them to array SOF elements adequately during times of asymmetric, diffuse, and episodic conflicts. In the next section, the authors explore the existing literature about strategies for engaging in asymmetric wars as well as the role of SOF. Further, the authors intend to demonstrate their understanding of these crucial themes.

B. Our Current Understanding of Asymmetric War Outcomes

The causal arguments of strategic theories, such as the indirect/direct approach, or the motivation to fight articulated separately by Andrew Mack, Ivan Arreguín-Toft, Jeffrey Record, and Patricia Sullivan, demonstrate the challenges of fighting asymmetric wars. The authors of this study take the strategy literature as the departure point and focus on the marginal impact of improving the role of SOF in maintaining enduring relationships in current engagements such as those in Afghanistan, Iraq, and Syria. The literature review first discusses the nature of big states; second, highlights the military strategy of engaging in asymmetric wars; and third, emphasizes the role of SOF in this context to set up the importance of building and maintaining relationships.

Mack and Sullivan touch on the nature of big states in fighting asymmetric wars. Mack states that big powers often have to withdraw from asymmetric conflicts due to their lack of motivation and political will to fight.[19] He argues that big nations lack the political and

---

[18] Mara E. Karlin, *Building Militaries in Fragile States: Challenges for the United States* (Philadelphia: University of Pennsylvania Press, 2018).

[19] Andrew Mack, "Why Big Nations Lose Small Wars," *World Politics: A Quarterly Journal of International Relations* 27, no. 2 (1975): 175–200, https://doi.org/10.2307/2009880.

public support necessary to defeat insurgencies possessing a personal interest to survive and, therefore, stronger will to win. Therefore, Mack suggests that big nations should aim to win quickly and with reasonable expense. According to Sullivan, strong states are able to win when their target is to overthrow a regime or seize territory from a weaker side.[20] She highlights the relationship between the value of political objectives and victory.

Arreguín-Toft and Record analyze the military strategy of engaging in asymmetric wars. Arreguín-Toft claims "that strong actors will lose asymmetric conflicts when they use the wrong strategy vis-à-vis their opponents' strategy."[21] He argues that the direct strategy aims at the enemy's capacity to fight, while the indirect approach seeks to destroy the enemy's will to fight. Arreguín-Toft recommends that the strong should pursue the indirect approach of *barbarism and terrorism* to destroy the will of the insurgents to fight. Record argues that most insurgencies fail without decisive external support, and therefore, strong actors can defeat an insurgency if they cut off its external assistance.[22] Taking one of Record's examples, during the Soviet invasion in Afghanistan, the insurgent mujahedeen profited significantly from the United States and others' external backing, like the Arab volunteers who came through friendly Pakistan. It is impossible "to determine with certitude whether external assistance was decisive, or even whether it contributed more to the weaker side's victory than to the superior insurgent's will and strategy."[23]

Military and political leaders rely on appropriate strategies to determine the means, ways, and ends. The aforementioned theories indicate why Western nations fail to win asymmetric wars, including the war in Afghanistan that is now in its 17th year. On the other hand, they provide the necessary ways to prevent certain countries from becoming safe havens for terrorists. Reliable relationships, es-

---

[20] Patricia Sullivan, *Who Wins?: Predicting Strategic Success and Failure in Armed Conflict* (New York: Oxford University Press, 2012).

[21] Ivan Arreguín-Toft, "How the Weak Win Wars: A Theory of Asymmetric Conflict," *International Security* 26, no. 1 (2001): 95.

[22] Jeffrey Record, "Why the Strong Lose." *Parameters* 35, no. 4 (2005): 22–35.

[23] Record, 24.

sential to the indirect approach, compensate for the partner forces' weaknesses, such as the lack of combat spirit and motivation. From the coalition's perspective, relationships provide the needed lasting situational awareness necessary to adjust its strategy accordingly to reach geopolitical objectives. Within the military approach, the purposes and capabilities of SOF fighting unconventional warfare (UW) along with their partner units fit the strategic requirements of the indirect approach in current and future asymmetric conflicts.

Hy S. Rothstein, Anna Simons, and Lucien S. Vandenbroucke all highlight the role of SOF in this context. Regarding Afghanistan, Rothstein claims that *Operation Anaconda* in March 2002 was the critical turning point for the war.[24] He argues if SOF had maintained command and control of the war in Afghanistan from October 2001 onward, they would have assessed that it was an unconventional war, requiring a different campaign strategy. As Rothstein notes, subordinating SOF to general-purpose forces hampered the development of effective campaign strategies in Afghanistan because general-purpose forces produce only conventional solutions. In addition to this, Simons concludes that certain individuals already have an inherent talent for an UW approach of thinking.[25] According to her, individuals have either the capability to think unconventionally or not, and military leaders chosen to spearhead the UW effort should have the UW mindset. Simons explains: "We need individuals who see the forest *and* the trees, do not have to be taught to think in terms of branches and sequels, and do not need to be prodded by doctrine (or a President) to consider what the 2nd, 3rd, and 4th order of effects of an action might be."[26] She further argues that the design of SOF organization especially fits UW missions. Therefore, SOF should spearhead in asymmetric conflicts and be allowed to use their distinctive training and capacities.

---

[24] Rothstein, "A Tale of Two Wars."

[25] Anna Simons, *Got Vision? Unity of Vision in Policy and Strategy: What It Is, and Why We Need It* (Carlisle, PA: Strategic Studies Institute, 2010).

[26] Simons, 1.

SOF have experienced recurring problems, according to Vandenbroucke, who notes that "strategic special operations are also high-risk ventures for they seek to achieve difficult objectives in a single bid, with deliberately limited means" accompanied by "poor intelligence" and "insufficient coordination and cooperation between the services and agencies involved."[27] Linda Robinson argues that SOF are conducting more missions in more places than ever before, but the strategic vision for SOF has not kept pace with the growing demands for their special skills. SOF's main effort should be on "the indirect approach, a cryptic term used to describe working with and through non-U.S. partners to accomplish security objectives, often in unorthodox ways."[28] She states further that "SOF forge relationships that can last for decades with a diverse collection of groups: training, advising, and operating alongside other countries' militaries, police forces, tribes, militias, or other informal groups."[29]

The authors agree with the aforementioned strategies, but the focal point on the tactical level for a strategy to become relevant is missing. Formed relationships on the tactical and operational level have an impact on the overall grand strategy. Prior studies focused on the grand strategy whereas the authors emphasize the tactical level to determine the importance of enduring relationships and their impact on strategies. The tactical and operational SOF units, who train and work side-by-side indigenous partner forces, are the components who are critical in building relationships with those partners. SOF can be the glue between the Western states' geopolitical objectives and the local partner forces; however, without SOF's mechanism on the tactical level there will be no means to achieve any comprehensive, long-term objectives on the strategic level.

The role of SOF has continuously changed throughout time, but even as military technology and TTPs developed and advanced,

---

[27] Lucien S. Vandenbroucke, *Perilous Options: Special Operations as an Instrument of U.S. Foreign Policy* (New York: Oxford University Press, 1993), 4.

[28] Linda Robinson, "The Future of Special Operations: Beyond Kill and Capture," *Foreign Affairs* 91, no. 6 (2012): 111, http://www.jstor.org.libproxy.nps.edu/stable/41720938.

[29] Robinson, 111.

relationships continue to be a key component within the SOF domain. An evolving relationship between operational SOF units is required to ensure coordination and synchronization of training and mission execution to maintain Western geopolitical objectives and continued situational awareness. The following section highlights the importance of relationships, especially for NATO SOF.

C.   The Importance of Relationships between SOF and their Partner Forces

In the military and civilian world relationships are powerful ways to connect with others to accomplish any task, as exemplarily demonstrated through the famous inventor of Gore-Tex fabric, W. L. Gore. He notes that direct face-to-face communication works best in building, maintaining, and collaborating long-term relationships.[30] He states that he built his network of inventors solely on personal relationships. His relationships connected and "buil[t] their own lattice on their own initiative. This heavy emphasis on relationships extended beyond associates to customers, vendors, and surrounding communities."[31] Gore, who strongly believed that relationships are the vital key to any accomplishment, successfully built a global multibillion-business empire.[32]

The United States seldom fights alone, and U.S. allies have often been the strong partner in arms, as in World Wars I and II, the Korean War, the Vietnam War, Desert Storm, Kosovo, and during the GWOT where allies have fought alongside the U.S. military. In his study on global trends in 2016 affecting U.S. partnerships, Hans Binnendijk defines the historical importance of U.S. partnerships, and focuses on the anatomy and relationships of potential adversaries such as China, Russia, North Korea, and Iran.[33] He describes the

---

[30] Jay Rao, "W. L. Gore: Culture of Innovation," Babson College case BAB698 (Babson Park, MA: Babson College, 2012).

[31] Rao, 4.

[32] Rao.

[33] Hans Binnendijk, *Friends, Foes, and Future Directions: U.S. Partnerships in a Turbulent World* (Santa Monica, CA: RAND Corporation, 2016).

relationships between the United States and coalition force partners as the "outer defense," whereas partnership is defined as the anchor that allows international security, diplomacy, and economic institutions to "provide a degree of global order."[34] He further argues that "the United States relies on partners for legitimacy and intelligence cooperation, and for an array of mutual defense treaties and security arrangements that allow the U.S. military to operate globally."[35] Binnendijk concludes that relationships are fundamental for supporting partnerships throughout the world with those who help defend shared liberal democratic values.

Certain historical cases demonstrate the effective and enduring relationships between external forces and their affiliates that continued even after the end of conflict or war.[36] U.S. support for the mujahedeen in Afghanistan and Iran's relationship with Hezbollah are examples of such successes. Other cases had difficulties, such as partners simply having given up or taken their own advantages at the cost of their external supporters.[37] Some partners publicly criticized the presence of external forces or even turned against their sponsors by engaging in conflicts with them.[38] These cases demonstrated how an external supporter can lose influence in different ways. The partner can be defeated, which changes the dynamics of the relationship, causing a reconsideration of the terms.[39] The action of the partner or changes in domestic political conditions may force the external actor to disrupt the relationship. The partner may decide to desert or dis-

---

[34] Binnendijk, *Friends, Foes, and Future Directions,* 3.

[35] Binnendijk, 3.

[36] Idean Salehyan, "The Delegation of War to Rebel Organizations," *The Journal of Conflict Resolution* 54, no. 3 (June 2010): 493–495.

[37] Salehyan, "The Delegation of War to Rebel Organizations," 496–498.

[38] Daniel Byman, "Outside Support for Insurgent Movements," *Studies in Conflict & Terrorism* 36, no. 12 (2013): 981–1004.

[39] Fotini Christia, *Alliance Formation in Civil Wars* (Cambridge: Cambridge University Press, 2012), 43–45.

obey because of contrary ideology or objectives that developed over time.[40]

In an effective relationship, each side must be capable of aligning with the other's goals and ideology.[41] External powers have their own objectives and interests, along with ideological and ethnic identities that may be distinct from those of their partners. The main advantage for external powers to support affiliated armed groups illustrates the high-rewards, low-risk alternative to state-on-state conflicts or wars[42] with the intention to follow their own geopolitical objectives.[43] Further motivations of external supporters can be to build regional influence, destabilize other states or effect regime change, attack terrorist safe havens, fulfill domestic demands, or simply benefit from war itself.[44]

SOF elements are a part of an elite organization, highly skilled to build and maintain relationships. One of their most valuable and unique SOF capabilities is the ability to work with indigenous forces in denied territory and build relationships through their language capability and cultural awareness. The Mosul Study Group concludes in their report that a good relationship between partner forces is inherently important for any advise, assist, and accompany mission.[45] As in Gore's experience, the U.S. *Army Counterinsurgency Field Manual* (COIN-FM) points out that those relationships are the center of grav-

[40] Milos Popovic, "Fragile Proxies: Explaining Rebel Defection against Their State Sponsors," *Terrorism and Political Violence* 29, no. 5 (2017): 922–942.

[41] Byman, "Outside Support for Insurgent Movements."

[42] Seyom Brown, "Purposes and Pitfalls of War by Proxy: A Systemic Analysis," *Small Wars and Insurgencies* 27, no. 2 (2016): 243–257.

[43] Byman.

[44] Navin A. Bapat, "State Bargaining with Transnational Terrorist Groups," *International Studies Quarterly* 50, no. 1 (March 2006): 213–229.

[45] Mosul Study Group, *What the Battle for Mosul Teaches the Force,* 24th ed. (United States Army Training and Doctrine Command, 2017), https://www.armyupress.army.mil/Portals/7/Primer-on-Urban-Operation/Documents/Mosul-Public-Release1.pdf.

ity (COG) in any COIN operation.[46] According to the COIN-FM, relationships are the true weapon in any COIN missions, which "involves complex, changing relations among all the direct and peripheral participants. These participants adapt and respond to each other throughout an operation."[47] The interdependence between SOF and the partner force requires a certain level of interoperability and integration whereas the partner force is clearly the focus. The Mosul Study Group reports that "the quality of the advisor made the difference in enabling the partner force" to defeat ISIS in Mosul on July 9, 2017.[48] The relationship between SOF advisors and the Iraqi forces played a vital role based on the ability to coordinate and synchronize military efforts against ISIS. SOF's cultural understanding, training, maturity, competence, and empathy was fundamental in enabling and operationalizing the Iraqi partner force, which ultimately led to the victory against ISIS in northern Iraq.

On the downside, external powers have to take numerous risks when delegating war-making and supporting partner groups.[49] For example, external powers risk having partial or biased knowledge about their partners, which can have far-reaching and unintended consequences. To gain its objectives, a sponsor takes a risk when building a relationship with a local group that is incompetent or incompatible. Limited awareness may also contribute to a lack of commitment and will to fight among the partner forces, affiliate corruption and crime, over-commitment by the external power, developing possible support for the opposing side, and retaliations by the oppo-

---

[46] Department of the Army, *U.S. Army Counterinsurgency,* FM 3-24 (Washington, DC: Department of the Army, 2006), https://www.hsdl.org/?abstract &did=468 442.

[47] Department of the Army, 196.

[48] Mosul Study Group, 26.

[49] Idean Salehyan, David Siroky, and Reed M. Wood, "External Rebel Sponsorship and Civilian Abuse: A Principal-Agent Analysis of Wartime Atrocities," *International Organization* 68, no. 3 (2014): 639; Popovic, "Fragile Proxies," 924–925.

nents of the affiliate.[50] Therefore, U.S. SOF theorists recommend choosing partners who share a common ideology or identity and having linguistic and cultural experts extensively screen and assess those partners along with providing training and indoctrination.[51]

In sum, strengthening relationships can empower partners and allies to succeed. With and through their partners, SOF can prevail through resolve, resiliency, and maintaining continued momentum against global adversaries. The authors of this study aim to research the causal effects of the factors *constraints, training,* and *incentives* on NATO SOF efforts to build and especially maintain relationships with their partner force in asymmetric wars. By using case studies from ongoing asymmetric wars in Afghanistan, Iraq, and Syria, the study intends to demonstrate how these three factors directly influence the nature of the relationships and how the factors interact with each other. These cases demonstrate how and why NATO SOF units were successful but also failed in building enduring relationships with their counterparts.

D.   Research Goal

This thesis argues that enduring relationships are crucial for the success of the indirect strategy in current and future conflicts. SOF's ability to work alongside, with, and through indigenous forces in hostile or denied territory makes them essential in the indirect approach. Since 9/11, however, relationships between SOF and their partner forces have not always been properly built and maintained. *Constraints, training,* and *incentives* and their effect on current SOF approaches of building strong relationships are key components that play a vital part in leveraging those partnerships. This can primarily be achieved through persistent engagement and the integration of partner forces.

---

[50] Bryan Glyn Williams, "Fighting with a Double-Edged Sword: Proxy Militias in Iraq, Afghanistan, Bosnia, and Chechnya," in *Making Sense of Proxy Wars: States, Surrogates & the Use of Force,* ed. William Banks (Lincoln, NE: Potomac Books, 2012), 65–70; Antonio Giustozzi, "Auxiliary Irregular Forces in Afghanistan: 1978-2008," in *Making Sense of Proxy Warfare: States, Surrogates, and the Use of Force,* ed. William Banks (Lincoln, NE: Potomac Books, 2012), 89–94, 100–106.

[51] Salehyan, "The Delegation of War to Rebel Organizations," 505.

Relationships empower SOF to perform as a highly skilled and reliable cadre in collaboration with local partner forces to prevent and solve shared problem sets, accomplishing sometimes more with less.

This research aims to analyze the causal effects of *constraints*, *training*, and *incentives* on SOF elements' attempts to build and maintain relationships with their partner forces to meet the strategic objectives in asymmetric wars. The goal of this research is to explain how each factor directly influences the relationships between SOF and their partner forces to enhance operational effectiveness. The authors illustrate the significance of these factors and how they interact with each other. Using the cases of the military intervention against ISIS (Operation Inherent Resolve) in Iraq and Syria, and the war in Afghanistan (NATO's International Security Assistance Force and NATO's Resolute Support mission), the authors trace how *constraints, training,* and *incentives* were applied, resulting in different outcomes of relationships, which directly affected operational effectiveness.

E. Methodology

In this research, the authors exemplify the causal effects by using a structured-focused comparison methodology to show how the absence or presence of an independent variable correlates with the value of a dependent variable. Alexander L. George and Andrew Bennett point out that the disciplined configurative case study utilizes a historically important case "to exemplify a theory for pedagogical purposes."[52] The authors, furthermore, apply the process-tracing method of key variables as a fundamental tool for the qualitative analysis to illuminate the causal-process observation between the dependent and independent variables. The authors utilize the methodology of theory-building process tracing, which Derek Beach and Rasmus Brun Pedersen explain as a process "to detect a plausible hypothetical causal mechanism whereby X is linked with Y."[53]

---

[52] Alexander L. George and Andrew Bennett, *Case Studies and Theory Development in the Social Sciences* (Cambridge, MA: MIT Press, 2005), 75.

[53] Derek Beach and Rasmus Brun Pedersen, *Process-Tracing Methods: Foundations and Guidelines* (Ann Arbor, MI: University of Michigan Press, 2013), 16.

George and Bennett also indicate that "process-tracing is an indispensable tool for theory testing and theory development because it generates numerous observations within a case, but because these observations must be linked in particular ways to constitute an explanation of the case."[54]

In the cases from Afghanistan, Iraq, and Syria, the interaction between relationships (dependent variable) and *constraints, training,* and *incentives* (independent variables) creates the context for the analysis of the causal mechanisms between two experimental groups (SOF units), where the independent variable is changed, and the control group (partner force), in which the dependent variable is held constant. Each SOF unit (experimental group) is exposed to changes in constraints, training, and incentives (independent variable) over time, causing changes in the relationship (dependent variable), therefore altering the operational effectiveness of achieving strategic objectives. As illustrated in Figure 1, the first case involves U.S. Navy SEALs and Danish Special Operations Forces (DANSOF) (experimental group) partnering with a host nation indigenous counter-ISIS force, the so-called A'ali al-Furat (AFB) (control group) in western Iraq from 2015 to 2018. The second case relates to German Special Operations Forces (GERSOF) (experimental group) cooperating with their partner force, the Provincial Special Unit (PSU) (control group) in Balkh (BLK) province of northern Afghanistan from 2013 to 2015.

The authors selected the Iraq, Syria, and Afghanistan cases because they exemplify the most recent post-9/11 asymmetric wars in which NATO SOF were engaged to counter adaptable, flexible, and lethal adversaries. This area of operations (AO) continues to be a volatile and complex environment, challenging NATO SOF units to operate in. This study argues that *constraints, training,* and *incentives* can cause variations in *relationships* with the partner force, which ultimately influence operations and objectives, determining mission success or failure. While previous studies focused on military effectiveness, this research focuses particularly on SOF and their small, specialized units. SOF elements are cost-effective and capable, conducting and sup-

---

54 George and Bennett, *Case Studies and Theory Development*, 207.

porting operations in order to prevent strategic surprise, but foremost, to counter an adversary's action that frustrates strategic objectives. By tracing the complex dynamics of *constraints, training,* and *incentives* to predict strong and effective *relationships,* we provide insights into building and maintaining relationships that can be generated to enhance operational effectiveness; however, this endeavor will require further research and policy development.

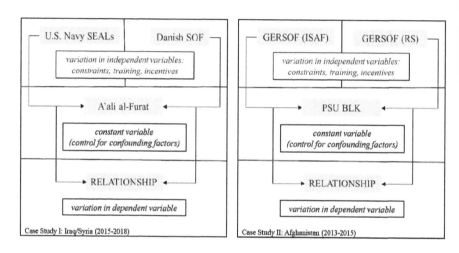

Figure 1.   Case Study Framework

1.   Constraints

Political and military constraints have limited SOF capabilities and complicated efforts to build and maintain the necessary relationships and operationalize those with host nation partners. SOF conduct operations in the most complex environments throughout the world, facing challenging strategic environments, but they also constitute an effective capability in conjunction with other irregular warfare capabilities.[55] Linda Robinson et al. argue that SOF have not always been "successful in making the case for employment of their capabili-

---

[55] Linda Robinson et al., *Improving the Understanding of Special Operations: A Case History Analysis* (Santa Monica, CA: RAND Corporation, 2018), https://doi.org/10.7249/RR2026.

ties to the policy making audience," which pertains particularly to NATO SOF.[56] Constraints such as a NATO country's national caveats, permissions and authorities, rules of engagement, national mandates, resources, or even a SOF unit's standard operating procedures, doctrines, and manuals have implicated and limited SOF's capability to partner with host nation forces in asymmetric conflict zones and small wars. According to Stanley A. McChrystal, budgetary and political constraints, furthermore, inhibited SOF's true ability to train, equip, assist, advise, and accompany host nation partner forces, complicating SOF's efforts to fully pursue national and strategic objectives.[57] Despite the constraints, the inherent demand signal for irregular warfare capabilities continues to exist in the tactical-operational environment as continuously seen in Iraq, Syria, and Afghanistan.

2.   Training

Training is a core task for any SOF operation. To meet mission objectives, extensive training is required, not only to prevent debilitating injuries or death, but also to enhance the operational effectiveness for any host nation partner force. One of SOF's unique capabilities is to identify, assess, and operationalize a partner force in order to pursue specifically directed objectives in times of war and peace. In every aspect of training, SOF plan for the unknown, incorporate contingency plans, and prepare for worst-case scenarios. This does not only pertain to SOF units, but also for their host nation partner forces. Building partner capacity and interoperability through training in fragile states, especially during asymmetric wars, has always been a challenge, but it is necessary to prevail.

Partner-nation engagement through training is a critical element for internal defense. SOF are deeply invested in ensuring that our international host nation partners have the experience and capacity to address threats and armed conflict, either on their own or in tandem

---

56 Robinson et al., xv.

57 Stanley A. McChrystal, *Team of Teams: The Power of Small Groups in a Fragmented World* (New York: Penguin Books, 2015); Jeffrey A. Builta and Eric N. Heller, "Reflections on 10 Years of Counterterrorism Analysis," *Studies in Intelligence* 55, no. 3 (September 2011): 1–15.

with NATO SOF partners. As Mara E. Karlin argues, "The United States has often responded to its allies' faltering internal security situation by training and equipping their militaries."[58] Yet, when and under what circumstances have SOF-sponsored training programs to strengthen partner forces succeeded?

SOF conduct training through bilateral and multilateral partnership initiatives with foreign host partner forces to enhance their responses to regional or global threats. Training engagements are critical, particularly for establishing a multinational response to threats like ISIS while serving as a bridge to broader stability and security among nations. According to a Congressional Research Service report, "the assumptions that building foreign security forces will have tangible U.S. national security benefits remains a relatively untested proposition"; furthermore, the report states that "neither the policy nor academic communities have explored in great detail whether or not Building Partner Capacity (BPC) works to achieve U.S. strategic objectives."[59] Despite the question of whether the Department of Defense-sponsored BPC program actually advances U.S. national interest, training remains a critical task to any NATO SOF entity.

3.   Incentives

Incentives are a key factor for decision-making, cooperation, competition, and motivation. The aforementioned Congressional Research Service report describes that "incentives for both the United States and the recipient countries to develop unified approaches to accomplishing military and political goals, thereby strengthening both the nascent NATO and U.N. organizations."[60] SOF use military and financial incentives to increase the allied NATO SOF participation including host nation partner forces to build relationships, enhancing institutional and interpersonal linkages. Incentives continuously play a

---

[58] Karlin, *Building Militaries in Fragile States*, 1.

[59] Kathleen J. McInnis and Nathan J. Lucas, *What Is "Building Partner Capacity?" Issues for Congress*. CRS Report No. R44313 (Washington, DC: Congressional Research Service, 2015), 1, https://fas.org/sgp/crs/natsec/R44313.pdf.

[60] McInnis and Lucas, *What Is "Building Partner Capacity?" Issues for Congress*, 54.

vital role and enable SOF to pursue limited or long-term objectives of national interest.

The SOF advisors need to use certain incentives to motivate their partner forces to gain objectives of interest, especially in fragile or failed states with partner forces lacking national identity and loyalty. Tailored to the partner forces, the SOF advisors can utilize a variety of incentives options to enhance their role with the aim to promote and enhance their capability to conduct operations. Incentives such as resources, finances, equipment, skills, assets, and status will compensate for the weaknesses of the indigenous partners.

4.   Framing the Factors in the Causal Mechanism

The authors analyze the interrelated factors *constraints, training,* and *incentives* involved when SOF build and maintain relationships to enhance operational effectiveness in order to attain strategic objectives in asymmetric wars. As shown in Figure 2, SOF intend to influence and operationalize relationships (dependent variable) through *constraints, training,* and *incentives* (independent variables) to improve interoperability and operational effectiveness of the partner force. The authors determine how the independent variable causes variation in the dependent variable, achieving different outcomes.

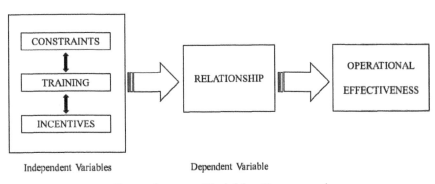

Figure 2.   Variables Framework

Beach and Pederson assert that "mechanistic understanding of causality is the dynamic, interactive influence of causes on outcomes and in particular how causal forces are transmitted through the series of interlocking parts of a causal mechanism to contribute to producing an outcome."[61] The structure of the case studies follows the factors *constraints, training,* and *incentives.* The independent variables interact with each other affecting the relationships between SOF and their partner forces, which influences operational effectiveness.

The two case studies for this research examine NATO SOF's ability to build, maintain, and operationalize relationships with their partner forces in Iraq and Syria during Operation Inherent Resolve from 2015 to 2018, and in Afghanistan during NATO SOF's shift of mandates from 2013 to 2015. Applying this framework for the case studies, we test the hypothesis that certain factors influence relationships, which are ultimately responsible for SOF's operational effectiveness in asymmetric wars. The degree to which SOF build and maintain relationships with a partner force determines the likelihood to attain the strategic objectives, especially during protracted conflicts, as seen in Afghanistan, Iraq, and Syria.

---

[61] Beach and Pedersen, *Process-Tracing Methods,* 25.

II.   THE A'ALI AL-FURAT AND THE LIBERATION OF AL QAIM, IRAQ

A.   Introduction

Beginning in 2014, ISIS conducted a multiregional insurgency to try to establish a regional caliphate.[62] This group constructed a sophisticated military campaign dedicated not only to expanding its caliphate from Syria to Iraq, but also to defeating America's Sunni allies in western Iraq while decimating the leadership of the Iraqi security forces. Craig Whiteside describes this as "the most successful assassination campaign since the Viet Cong's attack on the Diem government in 1959–1960."[63] In 2014, ISIS took over the cities of Tikrit and Mosul, and by mid-summer, engaged in the systematic killing of the Yazidis and other minorities across northern Iraq.[64] The true scale of this genocide may never be known.[65] At this point, U.S. President Barack Obama pledged to build an international coalition, placing SOF at the spearhead to dismantle and defeat ISIS.[66] The 5th Special Forces Group (SFG), responsible for military operations within the U.S. Central Command (USCENTCOM) AO, took the lead in Syria and established the Combined Joint Special Operations Task Force-

---

[62] Joby Warrick, *Black Flags: The Rise of ISIS* (New York: Anchor Books, 2016).

[63] Craig Whiteside, "War, Interrupted, Part I: The Roots of the Jihadist Resurgence in Iraq," War on the Rocks, November 2014, https://warontherocks.com/2014/11/war-interrupted-part-i-the-roots-of-the-jihadist-resurgence-in-iraq/.

[64] Nick Cumming-Bruce, "ISIS Committed Genocide against Yazidis in Syria and Iraq, U.N. Panel Says," *New York Times,* June 16, 2016, https://www.nytimes. com/2016/06/17/world/middleeast/isis-genocide-yazidi-un.html.

[65] Lizzie Dearden, "Almost 10,000 Yazidis 'Killed or Kidnapped in Isis Genocide but True Scale of Horror May Never Be Known,'" *Independent,* May 9, 2017, https://www.independent.co.uk/news/world/middle-east/isis-islamic-state-yazidi-sex-slaves-genocide-sinjar-death-toll-number-kidnapped-study-un-lse-a7726991.html.

[66] "A Timeline of the Islamic State's Gains and Losses in Iraq and Syria," PRI, February 19, 2017, https://www.pri.org/stories/2017-02-19/timeline-islamic-states-gains-and-losses-iraq-and-syria.

Syria (CJSOTF-S), training Syrian rebels to battle ISIS.[67] U.S. Naval Special Warfare, with its SEALs, took the lead in Iraq, establishing Special Operations Task Force-West (SOTF-W) and reporting to their higher headquarters Combined Joint Special Operations Task Force-Iraq (CJSOTF-I).[68] Other SOF organizations, especially NATO SOF elements, also deployed to Iraq. Under the coordinated command of CJSOTF-I, they supported U.S. objectives and contributed to the fight against ISIS, enhancing the capacity of Iraq's military and security forces.[69]

One NATO SOF partner joining this effort in Iraq came from one of the smallest European countries. Denmark deployed its national-level force unit, the Jægerkorpset, to western Iraq.[70] Known as TF-61 Danish SOF (DANSOF), this elite unit has been a steadfast ally of the United States since 1999. They partnered with 5th SFG during the early stages of the U.S.-led invasion in Iraq and Afghanistan.[71] This time, DANSOF partnered with 5th SFG's newly established Special Forces Operational Detachment-Golf (SFOD-G) 5426, the first post-World War II Jedburgh team operating in Iraq, to identify, organize, and operationalize counter-ISIS tribal forces in the Al Anbar Province. Even though DANSOF have very limited resources and a small number of skilled operators compared to U.S. SOF, this unit played a vital role, leveraging its relationships to operationalize a Sunni multitribe counter-ISIS force, known as the AFB, in the Al Anbar Governorate of Iraq. Ultimately, their effort contributed to the

---

67 Seán D. Naylor, "The Pentagon Ups the Ante in Syria Fight," *Foreign Policy,* March 30, 2015, https://foreignpolicy.com/2015/03/30/the-pentagon-ups-the-ante-in-syria-fight-iraq-islamic-state-delta-force/.

68 "Operation Inherent Resolve," Department of Defense, accessed May 23, 2018, http://www. inherentresolve.mil/.

69 "Relations with Iraq," North Atlantic Treaty Organization, July 31, 2018, http://www.nato.int/cps/en/natohq/topics_88247.htm.

70 John Sjoholm, "Denmark Deploys Army Special Forces to Syria," *Lima Charlie News,* January 22, 2017, https://limacharlienews.com/mena/denmark-deploys-army-special-forces-to-syria/.

71 Gary Schaub, "Denmark: Defense Woes in the Little U.S. Ally That Could," War on the Rocks, August 6, 2015, https://warontherocks.com/2015/08/denmark-defense-woes-in-the-little-u-s-ally-that-could/.

defeat of ISIS in western Iraq and to the liberation of the city of Al
Qaim on November 3, 2017.[72]

In this case, the author first provides a background of SFOD-G
5426, AFB, SEALs, and DANSOF units actively participating in the
fight against ISIS.[73] Second, as illustrated in Figure 3, this case com-
pares how the SEALs and DANSOF build and maintain relationships
as the dependent variable, with the independent variables of *constraints, training,* and *incentives.*

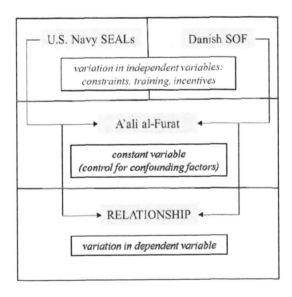

Figure 3.   Case Study I: Iraq/Syria (2015–2018)

---

[72] Cameron Glenn, "Timeline: The Rise, Spread and Fall of the Islamic State,"
Wilson Center, July 5, 2016, https://www.wilsoncenter.org/article/timeline-the-
rise-spread-and-fall-the-islamic-state.

[73] The following opinions and observations are mainly based on the U.S. author's
firsthand experience during his deployments as SFOD-G 5426 commander from
March 2014 to May 2017, supporting CJSOTF-S/I in support of OIR. The point of
view does not represent the official standpoint of the U.S. Army Special Operations
Forces, or in general, that of the U.S. Government.

By examining the same Sunni tribal unit trained first by SEALs and then by DANSOF, this case illuminates how developing relationships and specific techniques can differ when working with the same partner. Taking over from the initial effort by SFOD-G 5426, both SEALs and DANSOF operated from Ayn al-Asad Airbase (AAAB) located in the Al Anbar Governorate of western Iraq from 2016 to 2018.

The larger mission was to create one general-purpose force to counter ISIS's influence in western Iraq. First, the SEALs attempted to establish a small direct action (DA) surgical strike force, primarily focusing on individuals from three Sunni tribes—Albu Mahal, Albu Nimr, and Jughayfi. DANSOF, on the other hand, focused on organizing a diverse conglomeration of Sunni tribes, from along the Upper Euphrates River and the local areas between AAAB and Al Qaim. While the SEALs were using a direct SOF approach to build a small indigenous DA force in the image of SEAL warriors and equipping them primarily with U.S. weaponry and equipment, DANSOF used an indirect approach, working by, with, and through, using a train-the-trainer concept, providing their indigenous partner only with local equipment. They organized 32 different Sunni tribes into one coherent fighting element under the umbrella of the A'ali al-Furat while considering and respecting different intra-tribal dynamics, traditions, cultures, and languages. DANSOF followed a simple principle, best described about events a century ago by former British officer and Ambassador Alec Kirkbride as "duties were simple; I was to encourage the local inhabitants to stand up for themselves."[74]

Within the USCENTCOM AO, DANSOF's permission and authorities to operate were extraordinary due to the fact this SOF unit was not restricted by their national mandate or national caveats. Therefore, unlike any other SOF element in Iraq, DANSOF were officially allowed to accompany their partner force into battle. DANSOF's unique position to train, equip, assist, advise, and accompany their indigenous partner force helped them to establish credibility and trust among the tribal fractions who enthusiastically joined the AFB

---

[74] Alec Kirkbride, *The Awakening: Arab Campaign, 1917-1918* (London: University Press of Arabia, 1971), 104.

to counter ISIS in order to free their land and return home. The repatriation of tribes and family members in ISIS-occupied territory and the liberation of ISIS-held cities between AAAB and Al Qaim was the limited objective and end state of DANSOF's mission.[75] As Basil H. Liddell Hart states, "throughout history the direct approach has been the normal form of strategy, and a purposeful indirect approach the exception," and "often generals have adopted the latter, not as their initial strategy, but as a last resource."[76] The lessons learned from this case comparison contribute to a better understanding of the indirect approach, illustrating the necessity of partnership and the power of relationships. As Joseph L. Votel et al. argue, SOF's capability is to work "through and with local state or nonstate partners, rather than through unilateral U.S. action" to operationalize partner-enabled and combined missions against ISIS.[77]

B.   Background

This section provides a broad overview of some of the most versatile and unique SOF elements who were directly involved in the operationalization of the A'ali al-Furat and other indigenous partners against ISIS.

1.   Special Forces Operational Detachment-Golf 5426

Unlike the battles of World War II, the fight against violent extremist organizations like ISIS requires, as described by Maurice Tugwell and David Charter, special military forces and elite units most capable of executing "small scale, clandestine, covert or overt operations of an unorthodox and frequently high-risk nature to achieve significant political or military objectives in support of foreign pol-

---

[75] "At Least 25% of Al-Qaim in Iraq 'Totally Destroyed' after ISIS," *Al Bawaba,* November 16, 2017, https://www.albawaba.com/behind-news/least-25-al-qaim-iraq-totally-destroyed-after-isis-1049060.

[76] Basil H. Liddell Hart, *Strategy: The Indirect Approach* (New Delhi: Pentagon Press, 2012), 179.

[77] Joseph L. Votel et al., "Unconventional Warfare in the Gray Zone," *Joint Force Quarterly* 80, no. 1 (January 2016): 103.

icy."[78] The 5th SFG, known as the *LEGION*, played not only a "pivotal role in winning the first phase of the war in Afghanistan," but also contributed significantly to the fight against ISIS in Syria and neighboring countries.[79] In 2008, 5th SFG established the first 4th Battalion (BN), marking the expansion of an additional battalion for each of the five active SFG.[80] In 2014, however, the 4th BN was redesigned to better "confront, contain, degrade, and defeat unconventional, asymmetric, and irregular threats" in order to "meet future strategic and operational requirements in prolonged unconventional and irregular warfare environments."[81] The previous United States Army Special Operations Command (USASOC) commander Lieutenant General Kenneth E. Tovo points out that the reorganization of the 4th BN created "units of action designed to assist in understanding, defining, and preparing the operating environment."[82] Moreover, Major General Edward M. Reeder confirms that the "redesign of the Special Forces 4th Battalion pays homage to its rich heritage" from the Jedburgh teams and the Office of Strategic Services (OSS).[83] According to Will Irwin, three-man Jedburgh teams were responsible for procuring intelligence, coordinating supply drops, and providing liai-

---

[78] Maurice Tugwell and David Charter, "Special Operations and the Threats to United States Interest in the 1980s," in *Special Operations in U.S. Strategy*, ed. Frank R. Barnett, B. Hugh Tovar, and Richard H. Schultz (Washington, DC: National Defense University Press, 1984), 35.

[79] Dana Priest, "An Unconventional Soldier," *Washington Post,* December 23, 2001, https://www. washingtonpost.com/archive/politics/2001/12/23/an-unconventional-soldier/1ed14185-3b2c-4165-9d7f-5f4d9cc878c4/.

[80] "SF Expansion Begins with Fort Campbell's 5th Group," *Fort Campbell Courier,* August 14, 2008, http://fortcampbellcourier.com/news/article_075ef8cf-b7f2-5bc5-9044-4d87a2133228.html.

[81] Andrew Basquez, "SF Returns to Its Roots with 4th Battalion Redesign," *Special Warfare* 26, no. 4 (October 2013): 9.

[82] Kenneth E. Tovo, *USASOC Strategy-2035* (Tampa, FL: United States Army Special Operations Command, April 2016), http://www.soc.mil/AssortedPages/USASOCStrategy2035.pdf.

[83] Edward M. Reeder Jr., "Our Only Security Is Our Ability to Change," *Special Warfare* 26, no. 4 (October 2013): 4.

son duties between the resistance and Allies to organize, arm, and lead the local resistance forces during World War II.[84]

Charles Cleveland argues that the redesign of the 4th BN "is a deliberate investment by USASOC to build an enhanced, full-spectrum UW capability in support of the Theater Special Operations Command (TSOC) and joint force commanders."[85] Based on Cleveland's vision, the author was selected by the 5th SFG commander in 2014 to lead the first SFOD-G (5426) in Iraq to identify and operationalize tribal counter-ISIS forces to resist the expansion of ISIS's caliphate while directly supporting U.S. Ambassador Stuart Jones and the newly established Special Operations Joint Task Force-Iraq (SOJTF-I) in support of Operation Inherent Resolve (OIR).[86] Like William Colby, who parachuted into German-occupied France in 1944 and was "one of the OSS's most elite operatives, a Jedburgh officer to help the Resistance disrupt German defenses behind the Normandy beaches," the three-man SFOD-G 5426 team consolidated and organized a resistance against ISIS.[87] In 2015, AAAB in the heart of the Al Anbar Province, was surrounded by ISIS and considered the Alamo of western Iraq. Since 2015, SFOD-G 5426 organized Kurdish, Sunni, and Yazidi counter-ISIS forces in western and northern Iraq as well as in Syria to conduct guerrilla warfare operations against ISIS. As Votel describes, those operations were conducted against ISIS "to reduce their effectiveness and negatively impact the enemy's morale."[88]

---

[84] Will Irwin, *The Jedburghs: The Secret History of the Allied Special Forces, France, 1944* (New York: Public Affairs, 2009).

[85] Charles Cleveland, "ARSOF 2022 -PART II: Changing the Institution U.S. Army Special Operations Command," *Special Warfare* 27, no. 3 (July 2014): 6.

[86] Adam Taylor, "Why It Matters That U.S. Troops Are in Iraq's Troubled Anbar Province—Again," *Washington Post*, November 12, 2014, https://www.washingtonpost.com/news/worldviews/wp/2014/11/12/why-it-matters-that-u-s-troops-are-in-iraqs-troubled-anbar-province-again/.

[87] John L. Plaster, *SOG: The Secret Wars of America's Commandos in Vietnam* (New York: Onyx Book, 1998), 18.

[88] Votel et al., "Unconventional Warfare in the Gray Zone," 105.

In the summer of 2016, SFOD-G 5426 identified and assessed a multitribal group and its leader, who had worked with 5th SFG Operational Detachment-Alpha (ODA) elements in the past, to be the most promising tribal resistance force to counter ISIS's influence in western Iraq. SFOD-G 5426, however, did not want to repeat the past mistakes of previous ODAs, which had primarily promoted mainly one Sunni tribe during Al Anbar's Awakening, the so-called *Sahwa*. This had enabled the Albu Mahal tribe, known for their illicit smuggling activities on the Syrian border, in Al Qaim to engage "in open warfare against Al Qaeda in Iraq in 2005."[89] The U.S. military co-opted Sunni tribal leaders and trained and equipped the Albu Mahal tribe, which resulted in "aggravated armed conflict between and among ethnic groups."[90] Tribal engagement strategies were exploited for short-term security gains at the expense of Iraq's state building efforts because "the U.S. coalition had pledged to devote funds in support of the movement and provide *Sahwa* fighters with long-term employment by their progressive incorporation into Iraq's new security forces."[91] Nevertheless, "this promise was short lived."[92] The U.S. withdrawal from Iraq and the transfer of those Albu Mahal fighters to Iraqi authorities "were seen by many tribes as a betrayal by the United States," whereas "material privileges and authority by *Sahwa* leaders began to evaporate."[93]

From the beginning of the *Sahwa,* the Shia Iraqi government opposed the U.S.-empowered Sunni Albu Mahal tribe while critically assessing their alliance with the United States. Myriam Benraad describes how the Iraqi government looked "with suspicion and resentment, concerned that [Albu Mahal's] success on the ground might

---

[89] Gary W. Montgomery and Timothy S. McWilliams, eds. *Al-Anbar Awakening: Iraqi Perspectives Vol. II* (Quantico, VA: Marine Corps University Press, 2009), 12.

[90] Roberto J. Gonzales, "On 'Tribes' and Bribes: 'Iraq Tribal Study,' Al-Anbar's Awakening, and Social Science," *Focaal* 53 (2009): 105, https://doi.org/10.3167/fcl.2009.530107.

[91] Myriam Benraad, "Iraq's Tribal 'Sahwa': Its Rise and Fall," *Middle East Policy* 18, no. 1 (January 2011): 123, https://doi.org/10.1111/j.1475-4967.2011.00477.

[92] Benraad, 123.

[93] Benraad, 123.

translate into actual legitimacy and political power."[94] As the reactions of Prime Minister al-Maliki and the Iraqi government escalated, *Sahwa* members, predominately Albu Mahal tribal fighters, were first deprived of material and financial means, and then systematically repressed and their tribal councils disbanded. *Sahwa* members were persecuted, and as Benraad points out, "subject to arrest and held on terrorism or illegal-weapons-possession charges."[95]

2. A'ali al-Furat

Operating from AAAB, the AFB was established in the fall of 2016 shortly after SFOD-G 5426 joined forces with TF-61 of the DANSOF.[96] According to USCENTCOM's press release on March 14, 2017, DANSOF took the lead in creating "the first multitribe unit formed in Iraq" originally composed of more than 20 tribes.[97] Its Sunni leader, a native of Al Qaim and a seasoned commander well known by the 5th SFG, was most importantly respected and supported by the Iraqi government and particularly by the Iraqi Parliament. Additionally, he had great influence and was well-known by the majority of Al Anbar's Sunni tribes and especially within the al-Dulaymi tribal confederation, a Sunni tribal branch with more than 1,000 clans, also known, as Sam G. Stolzoff emphasizes, "for its military history and tradition of fierce warriors."[98] His father was a prominent government official in Al Qaim before ISIS executed him. This was the norm for the other Sunnis who refused to join ISIS. Many like him lost not only their homes to ISIS, but also family members and loved ones, particularly in the Sunni triangle of Al An-

---

[94] Benraad, 124.

[95] Benraad, 124.

[96] "A'ali Al-Furat Facebook Page," Facebook, accessed May 20, 2018, https://www.facebook.com/furatupper.80/.

[97] John Fischer, "Humanitarian Law in the Fight against ISIS," United States Central Command, March 14, 2017, http://www.centcom.mil/MEDIA/NEWS-ARTICLES/News-Article-View/Article/1111935/humanitarian-law-in-the-fight-against-isis/.

[98] Sam G. Stolzoff, *The Iraqi Tribal System: A Reference for Social Scientists, Analysts, and Tribal Engagement* (Minneapolis, MN: Two Harbors Press, 2009), 47.

bar.[99] To honor those killed, the name of the AFB, which means the Upper Euphrates Battalion, and its symbol (Figure 4) signify the collaboration and alliance of Sunni tribes, and their willingness to act in unity against ISIS.[100]

Figure 4.   A'ali al-Furat Battalion Symbol.[101]

To build long-term stability in Al Anbar, it was necessary not only to focus on empowering one or two Sunni tribes as had been done during the *Sahwa* in 2005, but to assimilate the concept of the al-Dulaymi tribal confederation, to mobilize, organize, and conduct combined operations with multiple tribes against ISIS. Local Sunni tribes willingly united under the umbrella of the A'ali al Furat, volunteering to fight in collaboration with their Sunni brothers. This band of brothers was composed of a variety of tribes and had the desire to support Al Anbar's 7th Iraqi Army to enhance legitimacy and share their burden in the fight against ISIS. The limited objective for the AFB was to liberate their hometowns and tribal areas, restore legitimate governance in Al Qaim and nearby cities, repatriate family

---

[99] Orla Guerin, "Iraq: Sunni Tribe 'left for Slaughter' by Islamic State," BBC, November 10, 2014, http://www.bbc.com/news/world-middle-east-29984668.

[100] Facebook, "A'ali Al-Furat Facebook Page."

[101] Facebook, "A'ali Al-Furat." Note: the A'ali al-Furat Symbol was developed by the A'ali al-Furat leadership in conjunction with DANSOF and SFOD-G 5426 in 2017. The Symbol is a representation of all the Sunni tribes that volunteered to jointly fight against ISIS.

members and tribes, and, as Sunni, reconcile and transition to support the legitimate Shia-led Iraqi government. The common goal to defeat ISIS set the exemplary conditions for the success of the AFB and their fight to liberate Al Qaim.[102]

3.   U.S. Navy SEAL Teams

Since the inception of SOJTF-I in 2014, the Navy Special Warfare Group (NSW) led SOTF-W and deployed several of its SEAL platoons to northern and western Iraq.[103] These SEAL teams were highly trained and tactically expert, skilled to execute the DA mission and conduct special reconnaissance (SR) utilizing a direct approach, meaning the unit achieves the results by themselves, neutralizing their adversaries in short duration operations.[104] SEALs are historically known to "act as naval commandos, whose functions were to gather intelligence, raid, ambush, capture prisoners, and create havoc in the enemy's rear areas. They could be used to instruct the forces of other nations in the same techniques."[105] SEALs played significant roles during several historic battles such as the D-Day landings when Naval Combat Demolition Units, the predecessors of today's SEALs, used explosives to clear the way for vessels and Allied soldiers. During the Invasion of Okinawa in 1945, Underwater Demolition Teams conducted reconnaissance and surveys in preparation for the landing of

102 "ISIL Loses Al-Qaim in Iraq and Deir Az Zor in Syria," *Al Jazeera*, November 3, 2017, https://www. aljazeera.com/news/2017/11/isil-loses-al-qaim-iraq-deir-az-zor-syria-171103185913263.html.

103 Andrew Grandpre, "Inside Mosul, U.S. Military Advisers Wear Black to Blend in with Elite Iraqi Units," *Military Times,* March 26, 2017, https://www.militarytimes.com/news/your-military/2017/03/26/inside-mosul-u-s-military-advisers-wear-black-to-blend-in-with-elite-iraqi-units/.

104 Rob Thornton, "BPC and the Indirect vs. Direct Approach in the Long War," *Small Wars Journal* (blog), accessed May 22, 2018, http://smallwarsjournal. com/blog/bpc-and-the-indirect-vs-direct-approach-in-the-long-war.

105 T. L. Bosiljevac, *SEALs: UDT/SEAL Operations in Vietnam* (Boulder, CO: Paladin Press, 1990), 6.

thousands of U.S. Army and Marine forces.[106] SEALs have proved exemplary in executing short-term and time-sensitive missions such as rescuing Captain Richard Phillips from Somali pirates in 2009 and aid workers in Somalia in 2012, but they are most well-known for killing Osama bin Laden in 2011.[107]

In 2015, SEALs from SOTF-W began to execute a concept, as stated in the Ronald W. Reagan National Defense Authorization Act for Fiscal Year 2005, to "provide support to foreign forces, irregular forces, groups, or individuals engaged in supporting or facilitating ongoing military operations by United States special operations forces to combat terrorism."[108] In 2016, the SEAL Platoon collocated with DANSOF and SFOD-G 5426 at AAAB received allocated funding, weapons, and vehicles intended to establish and instruct an Iraqi Sunni tribal indigenous force to fight against ISIS.

The SEALs faced certain obstacles and challenges to find, build, and maintain such indigenous element. Unlike DANSOF, which had experienced and seasoned SOF operators who had conducted missions in the Middle East and Africa since 2002, the SEAL team was composed of capable and well-trained individuals, but for most of the team members, it was their first deployment, so they were lacking operational experience. Those who had been deployed before had mainly operated in Afghanistan, not the Middle East. The SEALs' most notable challenges, however, were the lack of language capability, cultural awareness, and understanding of the Iraqi tribal dynamics, which caused dilemmas in training, mission execution, and, most importantly, during key leader engagements. The SEALs used a handful of interpreters who spoke the language, but were originally from other parts of Iraq and spoke a different dialect. DANSOF, on the other hand, hired only local interpreters and had capable team

---

[106] Sarah Pruitt, "Navy SEALs: 10 Key Missions," History, January 5, 2017, http://www.history.com/news/navy-seals-10-key-missions.

[107] Pruitt.

[108] Ronald W. Reagan National Defense Authorization Act for Fiscal Year 2005, Pub. L. No. 276 (2004). https://www.congress.gov/108/plaws/publ375/PLAW-108publ375.pdf.

members who fluently spoke Arabic, capable of communicating without any hired translator.

The SEALs replicated some of their own selection processes as the standard by which to assess, select, and recruit tribal fighters originating mainly from the Albu Mahal tribe, to include some from the Albu Nimr and Jughayfi tribes. Other tribes, especially the smaller tribes of the local area, were excluded. The tribal fighters who passed the initial screening underwent a selection process where they had to do push-ups, sit-ups, run, and conduct forced marches while carrying a heavy rucksack. This was all done while SEALs placed the Iraqi tribesmen under stress, yelling at and drilling the trainees in English. Those individuals who could not perform to standard gained some extra attention from the instructor and, in some cases, were corrected and disciplined on the spot in front of their peers. This method may be inadequate for selecting Arabs because the honor-shame dynamics are different in the Middle East compared to Western states.[109] Typically, Muslim Arabs live and die for honor; therefore, if a person is publicly shamed, it will affect his/her reputation, to include the family's status.[110] Public shaming will require the Muslim Arab to defend and regain his honor, and due to the group dynamics, virtues, and relational loyalty, to insult one Muslim Arab in front of others is like insulting them all.[111]

This commando unit, which was composed of selected Sunni tribal fighters and built in the image of the SEALs, was sent out unaccompanied in U.S. marked vehicles to battle ISIS by themselves. Detailed tactical rehearsals were unknown by the Iraqi tribal forces, and seldom conducted due to the time-sensitivity of ISIS targets. The SEALs had neither authority nor permission to accompany their indigenous commando unit into battle; therefore, their inability to integrate as a joint force sometimes resulted in the loss of trust. The commando unit carried an image of well-armed fighters hired to par-

---

[109] Stolzoff, *The Iraqi Tribal System.*

[110] Stolzoff.

[111] Jayson Georges, "Honor and Shame Societies: 9 Keys to Working with Muslims," Zwemer Center, accessed August 7, 2018, http://www.zwemercenter.com/guide/honor-and-shame-9-keys/.

take in the armed conflict against ISIS, but clearly distinguished themselves from other Sunni tribes and Iraqi military forces because financial compensation was more important than political interest. The SEALs' measurement of operational effectiveness was solely based on how many ISIS fighters were killed and how many bombs were dropped during kinetic engagements.[112] Future reconciliation and transition for tribal forces to support the legitimate Iraqi government were only secondary thoughts. Unfortunately, after this commando force sustained several casualties during a number of engagements, almost half of the Sunni tribal fighters decided to disband the program. Yet, some still saw hope in serving Iraq and joined the AFB in 2016.

4.   Jægerkorpset

In 2016, SFOD-G 5426 assessed the Jægerkorpset, TF-61 DANSOF, to be the most capable SOF unit to train, equip, advise, assist, and accompany tribal resistance fighters to conduct combined combat operations against ISIS, as compared to any other U.S. SOF or NATO SOF unit in Iraq. Their national mandate simply consisted of one line "to defeat, degrade, and destroy ISIS in Iraq and Syria" with no further national caveats or restrictions, permitting this national unit to accompany its partner force into battle.[113]

The Jægerkorpset was officially established on November 1, 1961 in Denmark.[114] Around the same period, Brigadier General Yarborough met with U.S. President John F. Kennedy at Fort Bragg, N.C., on October 12, 1961, shortly after authorizing the Green Beret

---

[112] Leo J. Blanken, Hy S. Rothstein, and Jason J. Lepore, eds., *Assessing War: The Challenge of Measuring Success and Failure* (Washington, DC: Georgetown University Press, 2015).

[113] Jacob Gronholt-Pedersen, "Denmark Says Deploying Special Forces to Syria against Islamic State," Reuters, January 2, 2017, https://www.reuters.com/article/us-mideast-crisis-denmark/denmark-says-deploying-special-forces-to-syria-against-islamic-state-idUSKBN1541RA.

[114] "Jægerkorpsets Historie," [History of the Danish Army SOF] Forsvaret, accessed May 20, 2018, http://forsvaret.dk/JGK/Om%20J%C3%A6gerkorpset/Historie/Pages/default.aspx.

as the official headgear for U.S. Army Special Forces.[115] Overall, this Danish national-level force has less than 200 operators, finite resources, and a very small military budget, which requires DANSOF to prioritize training and mission sets based on their national requirements.[116] The Joint Publication (JP) 3–05 *Special Operations* emphasizes that SOF are designed to execute operations "in a culturally attuned manner to create both immediate and enduring effects to help prevent and deter conflict or prevail in war."[117] As Christopher Lamb identifies, SOF are "flexible, sophisticated, and accustomed to non-traditional missions";[118] DANSOF embody the organizational capabilities to execute strategic missions, which require specific capabilities and skills. Even with those criteria and Denmark's premier SOF unit's small size, this unit was well suited to take on the AFB. Furthermore, DANSOF believed, as Arreguín-Toft points out, "that strong actors will lose asymmetric conflicts when they use the wrong strategy vis-à-vis their opponents' strategy."[119] DANSOF, a tier-one direct action commando unit, therefore, adapted to a more indirect approach with a strategy in mind, which Arreguín-Toft identifies as a direct strategy that aims at the enemy's capacity to fight while an indirect approach seeks to destroy the enemy's will to fight.[120] As Arreguín-Toft recommends, DANSOF used a combination of direct and indirect strategies to enable the AFB to win the war against ISIS. DANSOF used their versatile training to apply either their commando (direct) or

---

115 Janice Burton, "SWCS to Dedicate Kennedy-Yarborough Statue," United States Army, March 28, 2012, https://www.army.mil/article/76701/swcs_to_dedicate_kennedy_yarborough_statue.

116 Eric Sof, "Denmark SOF: Jaegerkorpset and Froemandskorpset," [Denmark SOF: Danish Army SOF and Danish Navy SEALs] *Special Ops Magazine* (blog), May 14, 2013, https://special-ops.org/sof/unit/denmark-sof-jaegerkorpset-and-froemandskorpset/.

117 Special Operations Command. *Special Operations,* JP 3-05 (Washington, DC: Department of Defense, 2011), I-1. http://www.jcs.mil/Portals/36/Documents/Doctrine/pubs/jp3_05.pdf.

118 Christopher Lamb, "Perspectives on Emerging SOF Roles and Missions," *Special Warfare* 8, no. 3 (July 1995): 2.

119 Arreguín-Toft, "How the Weak Win Wars," 95.

120 Arreguín-Toft.

warrior-diplomat (indirect) skill sets, as David Tucker and Christopher Lamb mention, to "operate with discrimination in complex political-military environments that are inhospitable to conventional forces."[121] DANSOF assumed the ultimate enduring warrior-diplomat role with the AFB in western Iraq.

Upon DANSOF's arrival at AAAB in summer 2016, the unit initially lacked a suitable partner force after the 7th Iraqi Army Commando unit elected to train with an Australian SOF element. SFOD-G 5426 identified and set conditions for the AFB and its leader to be the most suitable tribal force against ISIS. SFOD-G 5426 realized that DANSOF would be the ideal partner force for the AFB, capable of adequately training, advising, and assisting the tribal force.[122] U.S. President Obama's play-it-safe approach, according to CNN, limited the U.S. role not only in Syria, but also in Iraq.[123] Nevertheless, what factors contributed to the successful partnership of the AFB and TF-61?

Both the AFB and the DANSOF shared a common strategic end state, which was to defeat ISIS with an intermediate objective to liberate Al Qaim.[124] This natural fit of the partnership between DANSOF and the AFB ensured that both entities worked towards the same goal, which naturally reinforced joint efforts. Second, the AFB leader was charismatic and adaptable, familiar with Western SOF tactics, techniques, and procedures, but also politically connected to the Shia Iraqi government, able to directly influence Iraqi

---

[121] David Tucker and Christopher Lamb, *Restructuring Special Operations Forces for Emerging Threats* (Washington, DC: Institute for National Strategic Studies, 2006), 150.

[122] Austin Long, "The Limits of Special Operations Forces," *PRISM* 6, no. 3 (December 7, 2016): 1–4, http://cco.ndu.edu/News/Article/1020184/the-limits-of-special-operations-forces/.

[123] Aaron Davis Miller, "Barack Obama's Play-It-Safe Approach," CNN, June 27, 2013, https://www. cnn.com/2013/06/27/opinion/miller-obama-risk-averse/index.html.

[124] Helene Cooper and Matthew Rosenberg, "After Gains against ISIS, Pentagon Focuses on Mosul," *New York Times,* February 29, 2016, https://www.nytimes.com/2016/03/01/world/middleeast/after-gains-against-isis-american-focus-is-turning-to-mosul.html.

parliament members while being an honorable member of the Sunni tribal confederation. Furthermore, he had a profound understanding of national, international, and especially political, tribal, and coalition dynamics. Third, DANSOF established mutual trust and was willing to accept risk and vulnerability based on another's behavior and expectations. The unit was able to build a trustworthy relationship through persistent engagement with the AFB, using what Edwin A. Locke describes as ability, integrity, and benevolence.[125] As US-CENTCOM Commander General Joseph L. Votel emphasizes: "We must take care to build and cultivate strong relationships, here at home and abroad. We need to be responsive to our partners and always listen and strive to understand their points of views and priorities."[126]

DANSOF used a combination of trust and respect to establish a positive long-term relationship. This approach, in turn, enhanced the performance of the AFB through true immersion and integration into the Sunni tribes. DANSOF acknowledged the AFB as a long-term investment in the fight against ISIS. They provided quality military training because they did not see the AFB merely as a tool to conduct accompanied missions, but realized that the AFB had to be the driving force for any mission being conducted. DANSOF and the AFB understood each other's challenges, but both found a common ground focusing on what needed to be done with respect to the mission to defeat ISIS. This resulted in a partner force that was truly motivated, willing to participate in training with no pay and under poor conditions, believing in the long-term end state to free their country, and willing to reconcile and transition to support the legitimate Iraqi government. The AFB was also less inclined to view DANSOF merely as a supplier of goods, funds, weapons, and equipment in order to boost their own power and pursue short-term goals. Furthermore, the unique tribal composition of the AFB ensured a broad

---

[125] Edwin A. Locke, *Handbook of Principles of Organizational Behavior: Indispensable Knowledge for Evidence-Based Management* (Hoboken, NJ: John Wiley & Sons, 2009).

[126] Joseph L. Votel, "The Posture of U.S. Central Command," United States Central Command, March 9, 2017, 6, https://www.centcom.mil/Portals/6/Documents/Votel_03-09-17.pdf.

support throughout the region as tribal fighters were placed into leadership positions based on the individuals' learned military skills rather than their tribal affiliations, emphasizing the equality of each member of the AFB. DANSOF's ability to adapt to the Arab culture, use cultural nuances, and assimilate to tribal traditions during training and combined combat operations caused other Sunni tribes not only to provide generous support and send their best fighters to join the AFB, but also enabled the AFB to truly unite Sunni tribes in Al Anbar against ISIS.

C. Assessing the Impact of Factors on Relationships among A'ali al-Furat, the U.S. Navy SEALs, and DANSOF

This section discusses the three factors—*constraints, training,* and *incentives*—pertaining to SEALs and DANSOF, both working with Sunni tribal fighters at AAAB in Al Anbar Province, Iraq, from 2016 to 2018. The case demonstrates how these factors create the causal mechanisms in building enduring relationships by analyzing each factor chronologically and separately, concluding with the interaction between them.

1. Constraints

Political objectives can act as constraints on warfare and military objectives.[127] Nevertheless, political objectives are the most critical component to strategic war planning, determining how to terminate the war after achieving the ends in order to promote better peace. As Carl von Clausewitz argues, leaders do not "need to take the first step without considering the last" because wise leaders should start war planning efforts with war termination and backwards plan, keeping in mind what will enable the end of the war, what to

---

[127] Paul Schuurman, "War as a System: A Three-Stage Model for the Development of Clausewitz's Thinking on Military Conflict and Its Constraints," *Journal of Strategic Studies* 37, no. 6–7 (2014): 926–948, https://doi.org/10.1080/01402390. 2014.933316.

request politically, and who will enforce the peace.[128] Tactical commanders on the ground have to pay special attention to identify the ways and means necessary to reach the ends, but they are also required to adhere to the law of armed conflict, rules, regulations, and to the orders of senior leaders. Especially during times of budgetary and political constraints, NATO SOF commanders are challenged to coordinate and synchronize efforts within the alliances in asymmetric conflict zones.[129]

The United States' interest, however, in the role of its Nordic NATO allies, Denmark and Norway, has increased since the rise of ISIS in Syria and Iraq. Richard Bitzinger argues that because "past manifested criticism of Danish and Norwegian security efforts, particularly of their low level of military expenditures and the declining size and/or capabilities of their armed forces," particularly their constraints, NATO "should accept such policies for the benefits they accrue to the West."[130] The fight against ISIS has become a learning opportunity for all NATO SOF members because constraints played a key role in determining the value of relationships between SOF and partner forces. President Obama's mantra to secure the United States through building strong relationships with foreign powers was inhibited through a variety of constraints. As George R. Altman and Leo Shane describe, "[President Obama's] critics have accused him of trading a strong security posture for political points, and for allowing the rise of terrorists like the Islamic State group whom the wars on Iraq and Afghanistan were supposed to silence."[131]

---

[128] Carl von Clausewitz, *On War*, trans. Michael Howard and Peter Paret (Princeton, NJ: Princeton University Press, 1989), 584.

[129] Anders Fogh Rasmussen, "Security Policy in an Era of Budgetary Constraint," North Atlantic Treaty Organization, June 21, 2010, https://www.nato.int/cps/en/natolive/opinions_64563.htm.

[130] Richard Bitzinger, *Denmark, Norway, and NATO: Constraints and Challenges* (Santa Monica, CA: RAND Corporation, 1989), v.

[131] George R. Altman and Leo Shane, "The Obama Era Is Over. Here's How the Military Rates His Legacy," *Military Times*, August 8, 2017, https://www.militarytimes.com/news/2017/01/08/the-obama-era-is-over-here-s-how-the-military-rates-his-legacy/.

During the Obama administration from 2015 to 2017, some of the military constraints were responsible for causing mission creep and the inability of U.S. SOF to take the necessary means to destroy and dismantle ISIS in their early stages even though U.S. SOF units were deployed to about 70 percent of the world's countries.[132] Furthermore, the administration expanded SOF globally to pursue foreign adversaries.[133] Although U.S. SOF units like the SEALs in Iraq were allowed to train, equip, assist, and advise foreign partner forces, they were prohibited from accompanying their counterparts.[134] As Barbara Starr and Jamie Crawford report, "the basic military policy has been that U.S. troops should try to stay behind a 'covered' or 'concealed' position in order to not draw fire to themselves."[135] There were a few exceptions when U.S. SOF were permitted to accompany their indigenous partner force, but those exceptions needed presidential approval.

This policy created a hardship, not only for all U.S. SOF units who were used to training and fighting alongside their partner forces like they did in the beginning of the post-9/11 Afghan war, but also

---

[132] Nick Turse, "American Special Ops Forces Have Deployed to 70 Percent of the World's Countries in 2017," *The Nation*, June 26, 2017. https://www.thenation.com/article/american-special-ops-forces-have-deployed-to-70-percent-of-the-worlds-countries-in-2017/.

[133] Thomas Gibbons-Neff and Dan Lamothe, "Obama Administration Expands Elite Military Unit's Powers to Hunt Foreign Fighters Globally," *Washington Post*, November 25, 2016, https://www. washingtonpost.com/news/checkpoint/wp/2016/11/25/obama-administration-expands-elite-military-units-powers-to-hunt-foreign-fighters-globally/?utm_term=.e899ae59773a.

[134] Paul McLeary and Lara Jakes, "U.S. Works to Bring More Sunni Tribal Fighters into Islamic State War," *Foreign Policy*, June 10, 2015, https://foreignpolicy.com/2015/06/10/more-u-s-advisers-in-iraq-to-train-sunni-tribes/.

[135] Barbara Starr and Jamie Crawford, "Exclusive: Inside the Rarely-Acknowledged Missions of Two Navy SEALs Killed in Action," CNN, June 12, 2017, https://www.cnn.com/2017/06/12/politics/us-navy-seals-ryan-owens-kyle-milliken/index.html.

for the indigenous partner force.[136] The lack of the U.S. political flexibility to do what is necessary decreased not only the partnership capacity and discouraged the local partner force to conduct combat operations on their own, but it also allowed ISIS to gain momentum and rapidly expand into Iraq.

DANSOF's national caveats, permissions, and authorities provided an alternative approach to partner engagement. DANSOF's constraints existed primarily in resources and equipment, but their political determination to strengthen their military commitment to counter ISIS in Iraq and Syria, allowed them to apply the necessary means to achieve operational and strategic success.[137] Denmark's national caveat to "defeat and destroy ISIS in Iraq and Syria" without any further constraints immensely enhanced DANSOF's capability and interoperability to conduct joint operations with their partner force as compared to U.S. SOF who were restricted to training and supporting their partner force from the rear.[138]

DANSOF's ability, endorsed and sanctioned by Danish political objectives, to accompany their partner force, instilled motivation and enabled them to create a collaborative engagement among their partner force. Binnendijk characterizes collaborative engagement "as joint leadership with partners and by concentrating on broad common interest, such as maintaining international rule of law" to maintain a minimalist force structure while relying on so-called forward partnering.[139] As Binnendijk describes, forward partnering emphasizes meeting the partner forces' challenges presented by their adversaries, therefore, "it stresses alliance cohesion and building partner capacity,"

---

136 Alice Hunt Friend, "The Accompany They Keep: What Niger Tells Us about Accompany Missions, Combat, and Operations Other than War," War on the Rocks, May 11, 2018, https://warontherocks.com/2018/05/the-accompany-they-keep-what-niger-tells-us-about-accompany-missions-combat-and-operations-other-than-war/.

137 "Denmark to Reinforce Military Fight against ISIS," Defense News, April 21, 2016, https://www. defensenews.com/global/2016/04/21/denmark-to-reinforce-military-fight-against-isis/.

138 Gronholt-Pedersen, "Denmark Says Deploying Special Forces."

139 Binnendijk, Friends, Foes, and Future Directions, 11.

which also "implies much greater pressure on partners to carry their weight."[140]

DANSOF were able to find common ground, determining limited objectives such as to train, equip, and operationalize the AFB to fight alongside them to liberate Al Qaim. DANSOF's constraints in resources, equipment, and material identified the limits of their power, but they were able to compensate for those limitations by stimulating and accompanying their partner into battle while drawing more on the AFB's capabilities and manpower.

2.   Training

Training is a key factor for building up any partner force, creating interoperability, and increasing the chances of operational effectiveness. As Votel points out, the training for military operations should be carried out "by, with, and through our partners to accomplish common objectives," while building partner capacity and interoperability remains instrumental to building and maintaining momentum.[141] The coalition pressured ISIS on multiple fronts and forced this adversary to face multiple simultaneous dilemmas inadvertently. Votel, furthermore, indicates that "the strength of the C-ISIS Campaign is the C-ISIS Coalition" and "without the support of the Coalition, the by, with, and through approach would not be doable."[142] Training is the primary tool not only to prepare local forces for kinetic operations, but also to successfully operate with non-kinetic means on a cognitive battlefield of the 21st century.

The SEALs at AAAB primarily focused their training on kinetic operations, cultivating a DA-centric training program for their indigenous partner force to neutralize ISIS. Several millions of U.S. dollars were dedicated to train and equip a small indigenous strike force. This force received U.S. weapon systems, ammunition, uniforms, vehicles, fuel, and most importantly, they received financial compensation for the number of missions executed. Furthermore, under the train and

---

[140] Binnendijk, *Friends, Foes, and Future Directions,* 11.

[141] Votel, "The Posture of U.S. Central Command," 13.

[142] Votel, 4.

equip program, the U.S. military provided a large number of weapons and vehicles to Sunni tribal fighters who were willing to fight against ISIS, thereby preventing a major commitment of U.S. combat troops.[143] A relationship was established between the SEALs and the indigenous partner force solely based on material and monetary expectations. The interaction of those incentives in conjunction with training formed a group of Sunni mercenaries who were more inclined to exert power and self-preservation rather than work hand-in-hand with representatives from the Shia-led Iraqi government. The efforts to train and arm Sunni tribal fighters resulted more in arming local fighters and contributing to a general power struggle in the Al Anbar Province than providing proper training or teaching them to be self-sufficient and capable to operate independently under the legitimate Shia government.

Lavishly giving out weapons, ammunition, fuel, and vehicles, the SEALs primarily used their funds to incentivize Sunni tribal fighters, mainly from the Albu Mahal tribe, to fight against ISIS. This established certain expectations by the Sunni tribal fighters who perceived the SEAL platoon primarily as a caregiver and provider of material support and goods. In essence, this was a payoff to fight their neighbors. For each mission, those fighters expected payment and additional weaponry, ammunition, and fuel from the SEALs.

DANSOF pursued a more holistic approach by training a cohesive tribal fighting force to defeat ISIS, but by the same token, to support the legitimate Iraqi government. DANSOF integrated hundreds of Sunni tribal fighters and united a multitude of tribes under the banner of the AFB. Denmark's unique national mandate opened up a wide range of training opportunities, but limited resources and manpower did not allow for them to be realized; therefore, precise

---

[143] Joe Gould, "DoD's $1.8B Train-and-Equip Request Forecasts Chaos after ISIS," *Defense News*, June 1, 2017, https://www.defensenews.com/congress/budget/2017/06/01/dod-s-1-8b-train-and-equip-request-forecasts-chaos-after-isis/.

training plans and objectives were established to train, arm, equip, and operationalize their partner force over the long haul.[144]

DANSOF recognized the need for training of their partner force in kinetic and non-kinetic operations. They were aware of the fact that information operations were as important as targeting and neutralizing ISIS. DANSOF's experience in Afghanistan and Africa had taught them that narratives play an intrinsic and strategic role in information warfare because they provide a means to influence the level of morale and esprit de corps. Narratives have to go together with kinetic operation to enhance the overall operational effectiveness of any mission.[145] DANSOF realized that foreign forces should maintain a discreet posture, focusing their training efforts through mentoring and advising their partner force by using train-the-trainer methodology. To achieve unity of effort, DANSOF consulted with the partner force leadership and identified the most talented and capable leaders regardless of their tribal affiliation and started to train those selected individuals in the mission decision-making process, troop leading procedures, planning, and information operations and tactics—tasks that are comparable to a U.S. Officer's job description. DANSOF, furthermore, consulted with those leaders and identified capable tribesmen to lead small groups of ten. Those group leaders were considered the squad leaders who were responsible for those ten men. An indigenous C2 was established based on input from the tribes. DANSOF trained and worked closely with those appointed leaders, ensuring that both DANSOF and the AFB worked toward the same goal to liberate Al Qaim while reinforcing joint efforts countering ISIS.

DANSOF focused on the long-term goal to support the sovereign government of Iraq while defeating ISIS in Iraq and Syria. They refused to repeat past mistakes by U.S. SOF during the *Sahwa*, arming

---

[144] David Williams, "Ousting ISIS from Al Anbar: The Advise and Assist Mission of Task Force Al Asad," Marines, July 31, 2017, https://www.marines.mil/News/News-Display/Article/1262206/ousting-isis-from-al-anbar-the-advise-and-assist-mission-of-task-force-al-asad/.

[145] Thomas H. Johnson and Wali Shaaker, *Taliban Narratives: The Use and Power of Stories in the Afghanistan Conflict* (Oxford, UK: Oxford University Press, 2018).

and empowering Sunni tribes who then revolted against a Shia government, which resulted in sectarian violence after the U.S. military had left Iraq. In order to counter the massive weapons proliferation, DANSOF decided to establish a centrally located armory where all the weapons and ammunition for the AFB were stored. Those weapons were only issued to the individual tribal fighter for training and combat operations. Vehicles were signed out to the squad leaders and returned after mission completion. DANSOF were capable of maintaining oversight for all weapons and equipment while the leaders of the AFB sustained the accountability.

As a coalition force, DANSOF trained their partner force not only on military tasks but also on international laws to protect civilians, wounded enemies, and prisoners of war. The AFB became the first indigenous organization that received training on the Law of Armed Conflict (LOAC).[146] As Rob Powers describes, the "LOAC arises from a desire among civilized nations to prevent unnecessary suffering and destruction while not impeding the effective waging of war. A part of public international law, LOAC regulates the conduct of armed hostilities."[147] This training contributed to the AFB members' profound understanding of the international and national dynamics. The short-term goal to liberate Al Qaim, defeat ISIS in Al Anbar, and restore the legitimate government in western Iraq was coupled with the long-term goal of the AFB to finally live in peace with a Shia central government.

Members of the AFB were willing and motivated to participate in training with little or no pay and under poor conditions because of their belief in the long-term end state. The AFB was less inclined to view DANSOF merely as a supplier of weapons, funds, equipment, and goods to boost their own power base. The predominately Shia-led Iraqi Parliament, furthermore, acknowledged the AFB and its Sunni fighters, providing financial and material support to them. Other tribe members of the Dulaymi Confederation provided direct

---

[146] Fischer, "Humanitarian Law in the Fight against ISIS."

[147] Rob Powers, "Law of Armed Conflict (LOAC) -The Rules of War," The Balance Careers. October 27, 2016, https://www.thebalancecareers.com/law-of-armed-conflict-loac-3332966.

support to the AFB as well, boosting their training and enhancing their capabilities, which ultimately led to the liberation of ISIS-held territory in western Iraq.

3.   Incentives

Monetary and non-monetary incentives play a vital role to motivate and encourage an individual.[148] The SEALs provided their partner force with an incentive payment that was significantly higher compared to what an Iraqi soldier makes through his regular salary. In general, this top-up pay was much higher than anything the Iraqi military or the Shia-led government could sustain on its own. Furthermore, the SEALs partner force would cease their services and discontinue executing combat operations when their monetary incentives disappeared. After the SEALs discontinue the program or leave, this DA-trained force most likely will have to find new patrons who are willing to pay for the services of a well-trained strike force. This scenario poses the potential for bringing nefarious payers into the picture.[149] To be a member of a highly motivated, specialized unit represents another potential incentive for the SEALs' partner force, making it very appealing to attain an elite status during times when Sunnis are oppressed and disadvantaged.[150] The determination to be a member of this unit may also emerge from desperation and the hope of obtaining extra rations, funds, equipment, and better living conditions in order to increase survival.

DANSOF placed significant emphasis on building rapport with the AFB. Their mission was to enable their partner force to liberate their respective tribal areas within Al Anbar. At the same time, the DANSOF mission aimed to establish a mutual trust relationship with their partner force rather than provide them monetary incentives.

---

[148] James Hosek, *The Role of Incentive Pays in Military Compensation* (Santa Monica, CA: RAND Corporation, 2010).

[149] Austin Long et al., *Building Special Operations Partnerships in Afghanistan and Beyond: Challenges and Best Practices from Afghanistan, Iraq, and Colombia* (Santa Monica, CA: RAND Corporation, 2015).

[150] William H. McRaven, *Spec Ops: Case Studies in Special Operations Warfare: Theory and Practice* (New York: Ballantine Books, 1996).

DANSOF saw the long-term investment and quality of training as worthwhile and considered their partner force not merely as a tool that would enable them to conduct partnered missions; DANSOF realized that the partner force had to be the driving factor for any mission or training. Thus, DANSOF established a close working relationship, trust, and crucial loyalty. Their ability to speak Arabic and their familiarity with Middle Eastern culture was extremely useful, allowing for direct communication. It was the basis for a common conduit for sharing experiences, enabling DANSOF to integrate with their partner force. DANSOF shared their food with the AFB, lived in close proximity and shared some of the living quarters, and joined their partner force during recreational activities and fought alongside them shoulder-to-shoulder against ISIS during their movement to Al Qaim.

The most significant incentive for the AFB was not the inherent monetary value; it was the unity of effort and esprit de corps among those different Sunni tribes who were united under the banner of the AFB. The incentive to be a member manifested itself in the individual's honor and integrity by joining the AFB, making a public and outward impression based on the Iraqi tribal honor code.[151] This Sunni multitribe organization became well respected among the tribes in Al Anbar; even the Shia-led Iraqi Parliament acknowledged and supported the AFB.

4.   Interaction among Factors

The interaction effects among the factors of *constraints, training,* and *incentives* resulted in differing relationships between the groups, which eventually resulted in different outcomes and levels of operational effectiveness. Interaction effects occur when one factor's impact depends on the value of another factor. It turned out that in this case, the factor *constraints* had a significant impact on the factors of *training* and *incentives,* but *training* and *incentives* had no substantial im-

---

151 Peter A. Naffsinger, "'Face' among the Arabs," Central Intelligence Agency, September 18, 1995, https://www.cia.gov/library/center-for-the-study-of-intelligence/kent-csi/vol8no3/html/v08i3a05p0001.htm.

pact on the factor *constraints*. Both the SEALs and DANSOF worked with Sunni tribal fighters at AAAB in Al Anbar, Iraq; however, DANSOF's approach, and their application of the factor *constraints*, resulted in their mission success even though they had far fewer resources, less manpower, and less equipment than the SEALs. DANSOF's national mandate to degrade, defeat, and dismantle ISIS allowed the unit to train, equip, advise, assist, and, most importantly, accompany their partner force into combat. DANSOF's effort to build trust and shape an enduring relationship was advantaged by the unique *constraints* of national permissions and authorities. As long as the AFB did not liberate Al Qaim, DANSOF's condition-based constraints continued to play a major role in the interaction effects related to *training* and *incentives*.

DANSOF's effort of working together with the AFB demonstrated that the factor *training* particularly mattered when the factor *incentives* was present. DANSOF used *incentives* not only to motivate the AFB, but to enhance training opportunities and operationalize combat operations. DANSOF did not only fight alongside their partner, they also attuned themselves to the Sunni customs and culture by spending most of their off time playing sports, drinking tea, and eating food with the AFB, establishing trustworthiness by demonstrating integrity, ability, and benevolence.[152] The factors were used as tools to enhance the relationship through persistent engagement. DANSOF built trust and created an environment where both entities were willing to accept risks based on confident expectations regarding another's behavior. The AFB's *incentive* was based on the principle of establishing a mutual trust relationship and friendship, which could be counted on during operations, rather than by creating a customer and client relationship.

It turned out that the factors *training* and *incentives* had no significant impact on the factor *constraints*. The factor *training*, however, had a major impact on *incentives*. The AFB was less inclined to view DANSOF merely as a supplier of funds, weapons, and equipment because the AFB was self-motivated to train and to utilize the avail-

---

[152] John Blakey, "A Formula for Trust," Management Issues, April 27, 2016, https://www. management-issues.com/opinion/7171/a-formula-for-trust/.

able equipment for jointly executed operations. Their incentive was to have DANSOF as a partner who was willing and able to fight alongside them against a common enemy. The SEALs, however, who used a monetary-based incentive structure to drive operations against ISIS, experienced a less successful outcome despite using many more resources and funds as compared to DANSOF. The political constraints that made the SEALs unable to accompany their partner force into battle, as had been standard operating procedure in the first decade of the Afghan conflict, inhibited the SEALs from exerting their full operational ability. This diminished their trustworthiness, which affected their relationship with their partner. The factors *constraints*, *training*, and *incentives* intertwine in their impact in shaping relationships. As illustrated in both cases, the factors clearly determined the strength of the relationships, resulting in different outcomes and operational effectiveness.

D. Conclusion

Building and maintaining relationships with a partner force are not easy tasks. The SEALs and DANSOF are two SOF organizations highly capable of executing strategic mission sets, which require specific capabilities and skills. The SEALs who pursued a direct approach only were not as successful and cost-effective as DANSOF who focused primarily on an indirect approach, using only parts of a direct approach when necessary.

DANSOF established rapport with the AFB early on, which was a critical ingredient to the achievement of partnership success. Charles Cleveland calls this the "tenets and principles to special operations, namely to encompass, both the indigenous centric war fighting capability in foreign internal defense and unconventional warfare."[153] DANSOF's way of conducting their mission exemplified one of the values that the theory of special warfare offers, "primarily working through collaborative efforts with indigenous populations"

---

[153] Charles Cleveland, "Special Operations Theory Symposium Remarks 30 August 2016," *Special Operations Theory* 3, JSOU Report 17-6 (Tampa, FL: Joint Special Operations University Press, 2017): 13.

to achieve greater mission success.[154] SOF organizations like DAN-SOF are designed to execute operations "in a culturally attuned manner to create both immediate and enduring effects to help prevent and deter conflict or prevail in war."[155] DANSOF demonstrated that SOF are sophisticated enough to adapt to nontraditional missions.[156] This unit operates according to a small and specific approach, which makes it effective and powerful. DANSOF used opportunities to train and operationalize the AFB to end ISIS in western Iraq. DANSOF, combined with the AFB, reached ISIS's decisive point and attacked ISIS's center of gravity in Al Qaim, ultimately ending the ISIS campaign in western Iraq.

DANSOF used their professional, organizational, and interpersonal skills to build an enduring relationship with the AFB capable to project and attain operational effectiveness. They focused on their *constraints, training,* and *incentives* to promote and mentor independent anti-ISIS operations. DANSOF developed comprehensive AFB leadership capable of independently planning, executing, and sustaining operations. DANSOF instilled confidence in their partner force and allowed failures to occur without catastrophic results in order to help the partner force learn from mistakes and enhance the AFB's competence for future operations. DANSOF built rapport early on and established a trust relationship between them and the AFB, enabling the partner force to build operational capacity. DANSOF trained the AFB and exposed them to operations without the direct support of air, rotary wing, and ISR support, enhancing their ability to operate independently and without coalition force support. DANSOF did not select the mission objectives nor determine how the mission was to be executed. The AFB selected the targets, gathered intelligence, and conducted a combined joint mission decision-making process and planning. DANSOF assisted the AFB, ensured contingency plans

---

154 Travis Homiak, "A Blueprint for What is Possible: The Value in a Theory of Special Warfare," *Special Operations Theory* 3, JSOU Report 17-6 (Tampa, FL: Joint Special Operations University Press, 2017): 83.

155 Special Operations Command, *Special Operations,* JP 3-05, I-1.

156 Lamb, "Perspectives on Emerging SOF Roles and Missions."

64

were properly developed and implemented and that training rehearsals were conducted before any mission was executed.

DANSOF promoted a deep partnership with the AFB. Denmark's national mandate followed a multiyear strategy, and DANSOF's mission was conditioned based on the liberation of Al Qaim. The members of DANSOF were pushed and pulled from Denmark as needed for condition-based operations. The same DANSOF personnel rotated in and out of AAAB, allowing the AFB to work with the same individuals for long periods of time, which then established a positive rapport on the individual level. DANSOF, furthermore, played daily sports with the AFB members, hung out, drank tea, ate, and fought alongside AFB members against ISIS. DANSOF showed deep respect for the Iraqi customs, culture, and religion. DANSOF truly worked by, with, and through the AFB—often suggesting rather than ordering or directing their partner, while saving any criticism for private conversations.

III. RELATIONSHIPS BETWEEN GERMAN SOF AND THEIR AFGHAN PARTNER FORCES

A. Introduction

After 17 years of war in Afghanistan, the Afghan Defense and Security Forces (ANDSF) frequently fail to provide security to the Afghan people.[157] Furthermore, without assistance from coalition forces, ANDSF consistently fail to conduct coordinated operations.[158] The Taliban, Al Qaeda, ISIS, or other opponents reportedly control the area where more than one-third of Afghans live.[159] To take the initiative against these groups, the Afghan President declared a long-term plan in 2017, the so-called *ANDSF Roadmap*.[160] The main objectives of this plan are to continue professionalizing the ANDSF through Afghan and coalition efforts, with these priorities: countering corruption, improving leadership development, expanding the Afghan Air Force (AAF), and doubling the size of the Afghan Special Security Forces (ASSF). The latter have proven to be effective; therefore, "the ASSF conduct the vast majority of the ANDSF offensive missions."[161] According to Afghan officials, the number of army, police,

---

[157] Shashank Bengali, "These Are Afghanistan's Best Troops. The U.S. Is Backing a Plan to Create Many More of Them," *Los Angeles Times,* December 9, 2017, http://www.latimes.com/world/asia/la-fg-afghanistan-special-operations-20171209-htmlstory.html.

[158] Gabriel Dominguez, "ANDSF Failing to Extend Control over Afghan Districts, Says SIGAR," Jane's 360, July 31, 2018, https://www.janes.com/article/82111/andsf-failing-to-extend-control-over-afghan-districts-says-sigar.

[159] Bengali.

[160] Department of Defense, *Enhancing Security and Stability in Afghanistan,* (Washington, DC: Government Printing Office, December 15, 2017), 1–2, https://www.defense.gov/News/News-Releases/News-Release-View/Article/1397079/dod-releases-report-on-enhancing-security-and-stability-in-afghanistan/.

[161] Department of Defense, 36.

and air force SOF shall be raised from 19,000 to nearly 34,000 troops, with the support of coalition forces.[162]

From the coalition side, U.S. President Donald Trump announced a new strategy in August 2017 with the purpose of preventing Afghanistan from again becoming an international terrorist safe haven.[163] Meanwhile, NATO forces will continue to strengthen the Afghan security forces and government to fight against al-Qaeda, ISIS, Taliban, and other insurgents.[164] The new strategy's main effort is the condition-based approach, rather than the time-based one driving previous strategies, which underscores the commitment of NATO to support the ANDSF. In the time-based approach, the constraint of time did not permit NATO forces to establish a linguistically capable culture-awareness skillset.[165] With a condition-based approach, the Resolute Support (RS) mandate will allow NATO to have improved situational awareness, which will provide a better understanding of the importance of the Afghan culture to build and maintain relationships.[166] The effect of NATO members under RS should be improved through continued efforts to train, advise, and assist (TAA) the Afghan partner and provide more combat enablers on the tactical level. As part of the TAA mission, the main effort is to enhance ANDSF capabilities by, with, and through the Afghan partners, ena-

---

162 Bengali, "These Are Afghanistan's Best Troops."

163 David Nakamura and Abby Philip, "Trump Announces New Strategy for Afghanistan That Calls for a Troop Increase," *Washington Post,* August 21, 2017, https://www.washingtonpost.com/politics/trump-expected-to-announce-small-troop-increase-in-afghanistan-in-prime-time-address/2017/08/21/eb3a513e-868a-11e7-a94f-3139abce39f5_story.html?noredirect=on&utm_term=.aeaf0de95b29.

164 "NATO and Afghanistan," North Atlantic Treaty Organization, September 14, 2018, http://www. nato.int/cps/en/natohq/topics_8189.htm.

165 John Amble and Liam Collins, "How New Is the New Afghanistan Strategy?," Modern War Institute, August 21, 2017, https://mwi.usma.edu/new-new-afghanistan-strategy/.

166 Jamie McIntyre and Travis J. Tritten, "Jim Mattis Breaks down the New Afghanistan Strategy: The Goal, the Plan, What's Different and How It All Ends," *Washington Examiner,* October 4, 2017, https://www.washingtonexaminer.com/jim-mattis-breaks-down-the-new-afghanistan-strategy-the-goal-the-plan-whats-different-and-how-it-all-ends.

bling them to lead in the fight.[167] With the new Afghanistan strategy and the recent changes to policies, training the ANDSF remains one of the most critical functions.[168] By contrast, the advising efforts across the country remain incoherent and little has been said to address this issue.[169]

In 2014, a major mandate and strategy change were implemented in Afghanistan, with the withdrawal of most coalition forces and the transition from a combat-centric approach under the International Security Assistance Force (ISAF) mission to train, advise, and assist under the RS mission.[170] The purpose of this case study is to analyze the different outcomes of the relationship at the tactical level between GERSOF and their partner unit, the PSU in BLK province, under the *constraints* of these two mandates along with the effects on *training* and *incentives* in order to illustrate the interaction among these factors (Figure 5). In short, training, advising, and assisting Afghan forces can lead to improved relationships when SOF advisors can conduct TAA with specific incentives based on the condition of the partner unit combined with combat advising, in contrast to the time-based approach in previous strategies.[171]

This case study first establishes the background of both units, GERSOF and PSU BLK, followed by discussion on *constraints* for the German SOF advisors, the *training* of the PSU, and the *incentives* that

---

[167] Department of Defense, *Enhancing Security and Stability in Afghanistan,* 5.

[168] "Reconstructing-the-ANDSF," SIGAR, September 2017, https://www.sigar.mil/interactive-reports/reconstructing-the-andsf/index.html.

[169] Adam Maisel, "The Adviser's Dilemma: Endemic Challenges and Unrealized Opportunities in the Training Mission in Afghanistan," *Small Wars Journal* (blog), May 17, 2015, http://smallwarsjournal.com/blog/the-advisers-dilemma-endemic-challenges-and-unrealized-opportunities-in-the-training-mission-in.

[170] "Resolute Support Mission in Afghanistan," North Atlantic Treaty Organization, July 18, 2018, http://www.nato.int/cps/en/natohq/topics_113694.htm.

[171] The following opinions and observations are mainly based on the German author's experience during his deployments on the tactical level to northern Afghanistan between 2011 and 2015, which covers the shift from ISAF to RS. The point of view expressed here does not represent the official viewpoint of German SOF, or in general, of the German government. All translations from German to English are by the author.

motivated the PSU. After exploring the experiences with the PSU BLK from 2013 to 2015, the case traces the impact of each factor in creating the causal mechanism for building enduring relationships. The discussion includes a chronological analysis of each factor, followed by an assessment of the interaction among the factors.

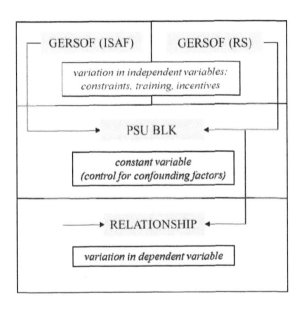

Figure 5.　　Case Study II: Afghanistan (2013–2015)

B. Background

This section highlights the history, training, and prevailing mindset of German Army SOF and their Afghan partners as it relates to the framework of the case study, followed by a general assessment of GERSOF's experience in partnering the PSUs.

1. German Army SOF

During the 1972 Summer Olympics in Munich, a Palestinian terror group took several Israeli hostages, all of whom were killed in an ensuing massacre.[172] Because the ad hoc German task unit composed of ordinary police forces could not rescue the hostages, an antiterror police unit, *Grenzschutzgruppe 9* (GSG9), was founded.[173] The unit successfully solved its most famous case, the hostage release operation (HRO) involving the captured airplane *Landshut*, in Mogadishu in 1977. When 11 German hostages were taken during the conflict in Rwanda in 1994, however, Germany decided not to order in the GSG9 after intense deliberations. Instead, Belgian paratroopers freed the German citizens, which revealed the lack of German capabilities. Therefore, the German Army SOF unit *Kommando Spezialkräfte* (KSK) was founded in 1996.[174] Their original purpose was to rescue German hostages in hostile territories where the GSG9 or other military units were not permitted to conduct HRO.[175]

The German decision in September 2001 to support the U.S.-led invasion of Afghanistan with SOF resulted in the assignment of the KSK to Operation Enduring Freedom (OEF).[176] GERSOF were deployed in southern and eastern Afghanistan to fight against Al Qaeda and the Taliban. From 2006, GERSOF operated mainly in northern Afghanistan under the mandate of the NATO-led ISAF until the end of 2014,[177] and afterwards, under the NATO-led RS

---

[172] Richard Sandomir, "Recalling the Terror in Munich," *New York Times,* September 2, 2002, https://www.nytimes.com/2002/09/02/sports/tv-sports-recalling-the-terror-in-munich.html.

[173] Jim Weiss and Mickey Davis, "Bundespolizei: Germany's Federal Police," *Law & Order* 58, no. 7 (2010): 46–49.

[174] Sören Sünkler, *Die Spezialverbände der Bundeswehr* [Special Units of the German armed forces] (Stuttgart: Motorbuch, 2007), 86–87.

[175] Sören Sünkler, *Elite-und Spezialeinheiten Europas* [Elite and Special Units of Europe] (Stuttgart: Motorbuch, 2008), 37.

[176] "U.S.-Led Attack on Afghanistan Begins—Oct 07, 2001," History, accessed November 21, 2017, http://www.history.com/this-day-in-history/u-s-led-attack-on-afghanistan-begins.

[177] "Bundestagsdrucksache 15/5996," [German Federal Parliament Printed Document] German Federal Parliament, September 21, 2005, http//dip21.bundestag.de/dip21/btd/15/059/1505996.pdf.

mandate.[178] GERSOF provided military assistance (MA) to several PSUs in northern Afghanistan.

Arreguín-Toft claims that the direct strategy aims at the enemy's capacity to fight, while the indirect approach seeks to destroy the enemy's will to fight.[179] Building on this, Liddell Hart argues that a strong actor should be capable of using both the direct and indirect strategy to win the war.[180] Therefore, SOF units, according to Tucker and Lamb, should be prepared for both strategic approaches by weighting their selection and training toward either the commando (direct) or warrior-diplomat (indirect) skill sets, which "allow them to operate with discrimination in complex political-military environments that are inhospitable to conventional forces."[181] To support an indirect approach, SOF should be capable to function in an enduring warrior-diplomat role.[182] In the case of GERSOF, however, basic and advanced trainings lack the components necessary to support a warrior diplomat, such as institutionalized language and culture training, or how to interact with indigenous forces in general.[183] The prevailing mindset and training are, due to the main and original HRO efforts, commando oriented (DA, SR).[184] Therefore, even after many years of experience working with Afghan partners, a gap in GERSOF's warrior-diplomat skills still exists.

In the German AO of northern Afghanistan, GERSOF teams have provided TAA mainly in Kunduz (KDZ), Baghlan (BGL) and

---

[178] North Atlantic Treaty Organization, "Resolute Support Mission in Afghanistan."

[179] Arreguín-Toft, "How the Weak Win Wars."

[180] Liddell Hart, *Strategy: The Indirect Approach.*

[181] David Tucker and Christopher Lamb, *United States Special Operations Forces* (New York: Columbia University Press, 2007), 150.

[182] Tucker and Lamb, *Restructuring Special Operations Forces for Emerging Threats.*

[183] Lars Werner, "Adaptive Reorganization of German Special Operations Forces" (master's thesis, Naval Postgraduate School, 2013), 33–36, http://hdl.handle.net/10945/39035.

[184] Timo Noetzel and Benjamin Schreer, *Spezialkräfte der Bundeswehr* [Special Forces of the German armed forces] (Berlin: Stiftung Wissenschaft und Politik, 2006).

BLK province based on the recognized requisites of their Afghan counterparts, the PSUs.[185]

2.   Afghan Provincial Special Unit

The ANDSF frequently use the ASSF as a striking force, with their capacity to conduct fully Afghan-led missions, including joint helicopter assault raids with the Afghan Special Mission Wing (SMW).[186] The NATO Special Operations Component Command—Afghanistan (NSOCC-A) provides TAA for the General Command of Police Special Units (GCPSU), which is the Ministry of Interior (MOI) component of the ASSF. Along with the Afghan Criminal Procedure Code, the GCPSU offers the capability to conduct high-risk Rule-of-Law operations, which include high-risk arrests and crisis response operations. The GCPSU suffers a high rate of casualties due to its employment in these situations, which results in challenges related to maintaining personnel and equipment readiness, higher attrition, and combat fatigue.[187]

The GCPSU commands 25 Provincial Intelligence Detachments, three National Mission Units, and "33 PSUs that operate in direct support of the provincial chiefs of police (PCOP)."[188] In practice, the PSUs are more responsive to the PCOP than to the GCPSU C2, because provincial governors and PCOP direct salaries and payroll systems for the PSUs. In general, these PSUs are highly trained and robust, which allows them to conduct high-risk, complex operations at the province level across the country.[189] The training of the PSU operators starts with the same basic training provided to all Af-

---

[185] Timo Noetzel, "The German Politics of War: Kunduz and the War in Afghanistan," *International Affairs* 87, no. 2 (2011): 397–417, https://doi.org/10.1111/j.1468-2346.2011.00979.x.

[186] Department of Defense, *Enhancing Security and Stability in Afghanistan,* 96.

[187] Long et al., *Building Special Operations Partnerships.*

[188] Department of Defense, 104.

[189] Joel Anderson, "Provincial Response Companies Train for Special Missions," DVIDS, March 29, 2013, https://www.dvidshub.net/news/106023/provincial-response-companies-train-special-missions.

ghan Uniformed Police. Additionally, PSU operators undergo a special selection and then attend a six-week course for advanced techniques. The foundation is advanced patrolling, which allows them to join an operational PSU. Once the new troopers arrive at their PSU, they continue training and refining their skills based upon each PSU's standard and their SOF advisors' operating procedures. When the troopers are validated to be combat ready, they are allowed to conduct high-risk operations that require the officers to make split-second decisions and take appropriate actions. These operations include high-risk arrests (initially based on intelligence from the coalition forces but subsequently shifted to serving nationally based warrants for known insurgents); HRO; recovery operations (cache recoveries of munitions and homemade explosives); tactical site exploitation of the objectives for forensic evidence; and security patrols.[190]

Unfortunately, the progress in many units, such as the PSU BLK, has been hampered due to misuse of PSUs by conventional forces and by their advisors, poor leadership, corruption, and lack of combat spirit.[191] These shortcomings, but also the effectiveness of the PSU, are reflected in the following assessment of GERSOF's experience with their Afghan partner units.

3.   General Assessment

In terms of the importance of morale in war, the ANDSF exhibit a significant and serious deficit: their weak will to fight in comparison to the insurgents.[192] After 17 years and billions of dollars spent, it is evident that if there is still no will to win from the Afghans, additional troops or money cannot turn the situation around.[193] Mason argues that the insurgents believe in their cause enough to die for it, while the Afghan security forces do not—a deficit that may be at-

---

[190] Anderson, "Provincial Response Companies."

[191] Department of Defense, *Enhancing Security and Stability in Afghanistan,* 105.

[192] Thomas H. Johnson and M. Chris Mason, "All Counterinsurgency Is Local," *The Atlantic,* October 2008, https://www.theatlantic.com/magazine/archive/2008/10/all-counterinsurgency-is-local/306965/.

[193] Mason, *The Strategic Lessons Unlearned,* 131–132.

tributed to a lack of national identity and loyalty. In short, Western allies have created, trained, and equipped the Afghan security forces who are simply not willing to fight hard enough or to die for the weak, corrupt, Western-backed and, foremost, illegitimate government in Kabul.[194]

On the GERSOF side, shortcomings were mainly linked to their mindset, training, and deployment cycle, which reflects their organizational and doctrinal limitations.[195] As already mentioned, German SOF's emphasis during training was DA and SR. The lack of proper training for cultural awareness and language capabilities made partnering even more difficult.[196] Years of training and readiness in counterterrorism and HRO created a professional mindset, which sometimes overused the abilities of the Afghan partners. It took time for GERSOF to recognize that fighting for the Afghan partners was not the right way.[197] In addition, the deployment cycle produced a new highly motivated team with the intent to make as much as possible from the deployment, which sometimes exhausted the Afghan partner forces.

The effort of the different PSUs in KDZ, BGL, and BLK mainly depended on the Afghan leadership and its relationship with their advisors. Strong leadership made a significant difference in operational effectiveness, and could compensate for the lack of national identity and combat spirit.[198] Especially in KDZ and BGL, GERSOF created adequate outcomes with effective relationships. The leaders of these PSUs were recognized among the other ANDSF, had the respect of their policemen, and had the will to form, promote, and develop their units. By building up and establishing the PSU in KDZ and BGL, the GERSOF advisors had the chance to put in the most

---

[194] Mason, 137–138.

[195] Werner, "Adaptive Reorganization of German Special Operations Forces."

[196] Thomas H. Johnson and Barry Scott Zellen, eds., *Culture, Conflict, and Counterinsurgency* (Stanford, CA: Stanford University Press, 2014).

[197] Johnson and Mason, "All Counterinsurgency Is Local."

[198] Karlin, *Building Militaries in Fragile States*.

time and effort for recruiting and training, which resulted in standing and reliable relationships.[199]

The PSU in BLK had less optimal results. First, the GERSOF took over from another Western ally that used different approaches. The PSU was already formed, which made it harder for GERSOF to build relationships with the PSU and to change certain personnel considerations. Most importantly, in contrast to the leadership in KDZ and BGL, a weak and unwilling leadership stained this unit. The leaders were not interested in conducting trainings and operations properly because this meant spending ammunition and fuel, which they preferred to sell for additional profit.[200] Moreover, the ties within the unit itself, where some benefited and others stood apart along ethnic lines, hindered the creation of a sense of team spirit.[201] Therefore, the difference in skills and efforts across the range of ASSF units was significant.[202] Compared to the other PSUs in KDZ and BGL, PSU BLK had the greatest weaknesses, was unpopular among the other ANDSF, was less effective in their core tasks, and, foremost, was corrupt.

Even though ANDSF were generally lacking morale and national identity, the combat spirit of the ASSF was distinct. But, only when their advisors and their "senior ANDSF leaders employ[ed] them properly, [did] the ASSF consistently overmatch the enemy on the battlefield."[203] The combined operations especially mirrored the effort but simultaneously the shortcomings of the Afghan PSUs. The German-partnered PSUs conducted successful operations with the full range of high-risk special operations (e.g., recovery of weapon caches and counter terror/insurgent/crime operations). The PSUs

---

[199] Markus Feilke, "German Experiences in Police Building in Afghanistan," GRIPS Policy Research Center, no. 10-02 (January 2010): 1–26, http://www.grips.ac.jp/r-center/wp-content/uploads/10-02.pdf.

[200] Arne Schröer, "Lessons Learned? German Security Policy and the War in Afghanistan," *German Politics* 23, no. 1-2 (2014): 1–25, https://doi.org/10.1080/09644008.2014.916691.

[201] McChrystal, *Team of Teams: The Power of Small Groups in a Fragmented World.*

[202] Department of Defense, *Enhancing Security and Stability in Afghanistan.*

[203] Department of Defense, 47.

were able to react on short notice for time-sensitive missions and conducted pre-planned, combined, and joint large-scale operations with conventional forces and other special forces over numerous days by using all available means of transportation. Due to the increased need for more Afghans in proportion to German operators to obtain the higher command's approval and the change to Afghan intelligence driven operations, the PSU leaders used more and more of the German abilities and assets for their purpose. In short, most of the operations had adequate short-term achievements, but limited sustainable effects, because Afghan forces could only maintain security as long as they remained in the area and coalition forces assisted them.[204]

The aforementioned lack of national identity and low combat spirit of the Afghan partner force along with GERSOF's shortcomings will not be the focus of this study, but it is necessary to understand the prevalent Afghan and German mindsets about what their relationship could accomplish and what standard could be maintained. This sets the baseline for the following analysis.

C.   Assessing the Impact of Factors on Relationships between German SOF and the Provincial Special   Unit in Balkh

This section discusses the three factors: *constraints* for the GERSOF advisors, the *training* of the PSU, and the *incentives* to motivate the PSU, by examining the German experiences with the PSU BLK from 2013 to 2015. The case study demonstrates how these factors create the causal mechanisms for building enduring relationships. The discussion analyzes each factor chronologically and concludes with an analysis of the interactions among them.

1.   Constraints

The primary objective of ISAF was "to ensure that Afghanistan would never again become a safe haven for terrorists" by maintaining security through enabling and developing Afghan security forces

---

[204] John L. Cook, *Afghanistan: The Perfect Failure* (Bloomington, IN: Xlibris Corporation, 2012).

across the country.[205] At the end of 2014, when the ISAF mission was completed, the Afghan forces assumed full security responsibility. On January 1, 2015, RS replaced ISAF with the main goal to provide TAA to ANDSF, enhancing their capabilities and manpower.[206] The number of German soldiers in Afghanistan declined after its peak in 2011 from over 5,000 to 1,300 at the end of 2014 in preparation for RS, which allowed a maximum of about 1,000 soldiers.[207] GERSOF advisors and support personnel declined in a similar ratio. To be prepared for the RS mandate, the last deployment rotation of 2014 rehearsed the conditions in advance, regarding allowed personnel, tactics, and procedures. The direct influences shaping how GERSOF worked with the partner unit were the time-based reports generated at different steps until an *independent* operating PSU; the withdrawal of coalition forces, which resulted in fewer available air assets, especially those for medical evacuation (MEDEVAC) to cover the *golden hour* rule; and the shift from combat-centric to non-combat TAA.

For coalition forces, the caveat under ISAF and RS was to treat their critically injured troops within the so-called *golden hour.* This refers to the period of time after an injury during which medical and surgical treatment has the highest likelihood of preventing death.[208] In Afghanistan, more troops survived life-threatening injuries through the extraction of wounded personnel, foremost by helicopters (Air MEDEVAC), within 60 minutes.[209] Therefore, the AO was limited to

[205] "ISAF's Mission in Afghanistan (2001–2014)," North Atlantic Treaty Organization, September 1, 2015, http://www.nato.int/cps/en/natohq/topics_ 69366. htm.

[206] "NATO Resolute Support History," Resolute Support Afghanistan, accessed September 15, 2018, https://rs.nato.int/about-us/history/isaf-history.aspx.

[207] "Deutscher Bundestag -Resolute Support Mission," German Federal Parliament, accessed May 2, 2018, https://www.bundestag.de/ausschuesse/ ausschuesse18/a12/auslandseinsaetze/auslandseinsaetze/rsm/363988.

[208] John Campbell, *International Trauma Life Support for Emergency Care Providers* (London: Pearson Education, 2013), 11–16.

[209] Patricia Kime, "'Golden Hour' Policy Saved U.S. Lives in Afghanistan," Armed Services Blood Program, October 5, 2015, http://www.militaryblood.dod. mil/ ViewContent.aspx?con_id_pk=1968&fr=hs.

the 60-minute radius of these bases (or forward deployed) where Air MEDEVAC was available.[210]

Even when the PSU was rated *fully capable of unilateral operations*, the advisors were continuously required to provide adequate combat advising in order for them to be successful. That included leading them to the objective, performing medical evacuation, in extremis support, or coordinating properly with other ANDSF during complex operations. The known end-date of the withdrawal and ISAF itself set a timeframe for the GERSOF to report the PSU systematically to *fully operational independence* by the end of 2014. Even when the true assessment of the unit was worse than the required standards, the German advisors reported the skills of the PSU according to the timeframe. The ratio of Afghan PSU troopers to GERSOF advisors shifted towards nearly unilateral Afghan missions at the end of ISAF. Independence of the PSU itself was desired, but only if they were truly independent and capable of fulfilling their mission sets. If Afghanistan was truly at that point, then advisors would not be required to assist their Afghan counterparts on the tactical level anymore, which the latest strategy actually demands. Major insurgent attacks from 2015 in northern Afghanistan proved that the majority of ANDSF units were not yet as professional, independent, and self-sustainable, as had been often reported against an advisor's conscience, to provide security to the Afghan people.[211] For example, contrary to the assurances by Afghan and coalition officials that ANDSF could protect the most important cities, the Taliban forces were able to capture, and shortly hold, Kunduz City in September 2015.[212] Army and police special units, advised and supported by NATO SOF, regained the city later on.

---

[210] Andrew M. Seaman, "U.S. Military 'Golden Hour' Rule Saved Lives," Reuters, September 30, 2015, https://www.reuters.com/article/us-health-trauma-transport/u-s-military-golden-hour-rule-saved-lives-idUSKCN0RU31F20150930.

[211] Thomas Doherty, "Letting Them Scrape a Knee: Advising for Third Order Effects," *Small Wars Journal,* accessed May 3, 2018, http://smallwarsjournal.com/jrnl/art/letting-them-scrape-a-knee-advising-for-third-order-effects#i2.

[212] Goldstein and Mashal. "Taliban Fighters Capture Kunduz City."

Constraints on the use of force did not allow GERSOF to deploy their capabilities to full effect.[213] During the shift from ISAF to RS, GERSOF advisors were more and more restricted from accompanying ANDSF into battle, to the point that GERSOF were no longer allowed to directly assist in combat missions at all.[214] A certain force ratio had to be maintained between Afghan and coalition forces in order to obtain mission approval. At the beginning, an advisor team was next to each maneuver element, and when no shots were fired, the missions were conducted as scheduled. Combined operations in hotspots often provoked firefights, and most of the PSU troopers were not willing and sometimes not able to return fire properly under stress, which resulted in so-called *green-on-blue* casualties.[215] The advisor teams could count on neither the Afghan capabilities nor, more importantly, their combat spirit to act properly under duress and fire. At the end of ISAF, due to the constraints, the PSU's steps toward independence, and the *green-on-blue* incidents, in particular, only one German mission element with its own force protection assisted the Afghan ground force commander (GFC). Only in extremis did the German GFC take over the lead. The advisors, however, remained at a safe distance during combat operations and were required to take position at the last covered and concealed position, directing and advising the Afghans from far away.[216]

When RS finally became effective at the beginning of 2015, directives of the NATO made combat advising nearly impossible. The effectiveness of the still ongoing training, and the advice and assist provided during key leader engagement (KLE), relied from that point on the reports of the PSU itself without advisors witnessing first-hand the operation itself. Yet, time spent and trust earned through shared

---

[213] Timo Behr, "Germany and Regional Command-North: ISAF's Weakest Link?," in *Statebuilding in Afghanistan: Multinational Contributions to Reconstruction,* ed. Nik Hynek and Péter Marton, 42–64 (New York: Routledge, 2011).

[214] SIGAR, "Reconstructing-the-ANDSF."

[215] Billy Roggio and Lisa Lundquist, "Green-on-Blue Attacks in Afghanistan: The Data," *Long War Journal,* last modified June 17, 2017, http://www.longwarjournal.org/archives/2012/08/green-on-blue_attack.php.

[216] Farrell, Osinga, and Russell, *Military Adaptation in Afghanistan.*

experiences—on the battlefield, if possible—is necessary to build and maintain human connections.[217]

The withdrawal of coalition forces and their assets had a direct influence on the ability to maintain the MEDEVAC coverage in northern Afghanistan. The GERSOF teams had fewer and fewer possibilities to advise, assist, and accompany the PSU directly when they were operating outside the golden-hour range. After the withdrawal from KDZ and BGL, only BLK province had Air MEDEVAC capability in northern Afghanistan. Only with sufficient advanced notice was it possible to request one of the rare but highly mobile Special Operations Surgical Teams (SOST) teams to build up a temporary coverage. Moreover, due to intelligence-driven and often time-sensitive nature of PSU missions, the advisors had fewer chances to accompany their partner during missions, which soon became a moot issue when the RS replaced the ISAF mandate.

The comparison of the factor *constraints* across ISAF and RS demonstrates three main changes with direct influence on how GERSOF worked with the partner unit. First, change resulted from the introduction of time-based reports generated at different steps leading up to an *independent* operating PSU. Second, the withdrawal of coalition forces resulted in fewer available air assets, especially those for Air MEDEVAC to fulfill the *golden hour* rule. Third, a major influence was the shift from combat-centric to non-combat advising. Hence, the assets and possibilities to operate under ISAF could have complemented the condition-based advising approach of the RS mandate.

2.   Training

The ISAF mandate gave the advisors more possibilities to TAA, given the circumstances in Afghanistan, than under RS. GERSOF advisors often deliberately violated the principle that the advisors should refrain from becoming the coordinators for their counterparts because the advisors' effectiveness decreases when forced into this role.[218] However, as already mentioned, to train and fight with a unit

---

[217] Maisel, "The Adviser's Dilemma."

[218] Doherty, "Letting Them Scrape a Knee: Advising for Third Order Effects."

80

lacking national loyalty and proper combat spirit, the advisors had to accommodate the Afghan system and mindset as far as needed to maintain a minimum standard. The restrictions of the RS mandate influenced the training of the PSU in regards to the permissible number of SOF advisors, the focus and main effort of the training, and foremost the application of the training on the battlefield.

The focus of the training on the individual, team, and platoon levels, and, at the end of ISAF, the shift to PSU command and control influenced the relationship with the Afghan partners. The individual and team levels required considerably more GERSOF advisors, a factor permitted under ISAF. At the beginning, the advisors had the primary responsibility for ensuring that training was performed for the PSU, enabling them to directly intervene against insurgents and to identify their strengths and weaknesses. During operations, GERSOF advisors trained, advised, and assisted their counterparts, preventing potential operational failures. GERSOF adjusted training as needed to enhance the PSU's combat effectiveness through direct feedback of performance. The saying that *nothing bonds more than blood and sweat* could be seen through the different steps, from the theory in the classroom, over the training area, to the battlefield.

Under the time-based approach, reports generated at the different steps of the PSU's migration toward independence frequently did not accurately reflect the true abilities of the PSU.[219] Even so, the advisors had to move on to the platoon and company levels, which weakened the relationships with the individual troopers who were no longer mentored. From then on, the PSU was autonomous and had complete responsibility for its own training and operations; the advisors assisted and advised the efforts and prevented only catastrophic failure on the battlefield. The focus on TAA of the C2 structure and staff personnel right up to the PCOP under RS made relationships with the key functions possible, but without reliable feedback about the implementation in real-world operations, the advisors' ability to assess effectiveness was limited.[220] Another advantage of tactical mis-

---

[219] Daniel L. Davis, "Truth, Lies, and Afghanistan," *Armed Forces Journal*, February 1, 2012, http://armedforcesjournal.com/truth-lies-and-afghanistan/.

[220] Thornton, "BPC and the Indirect vs. Direct Approach."

sion sets was the ability to restore confidence among the members of the security forces. More importantly, those units were in a position to demonstrate to the Afghan people that they were able to provide safety and security to Afghan citizens.

The disconnected strategy of TAA manifested itself most within the consistently marginal executions of operations.[221] Badly executed operations with human rights violations, failure to follow Afghan rule of law, or civilian casualties could taint hard-won gains. Therefore, it was essential to tailor missions to the ability of the unit to ensure the PSU built on the previous operation. In theory, when the advisors were working with the whole C2 structure of the PSU to plan missions, they could expect partner leadership would implement the plan accordingly. Yet, on the battlefield, the PSU did not consistently conduct the operation as planned, despite the participation and agreement of the unit's C2 structure during planning. The best relationship within the leadership was nearly useless if the men on the ground failed to execute the operation. TAA without going on mission was hard to sell and did little to enhance morale within the Afghan partner force or in the mentor team itself. Without proper integration and a show of commitment, it was nearly impossible for the GERSOF to build trust, credibility, and therefore a sustainable relationship with the partner force, especially when missions were not jointly executed.[222] Only then were the mentors able to assess the abilities of the partner force.[223] On the other hand, the self-assessment of the PSU was not reliable, and the training results were also not convincing. Numerous unsuccessful attempts to demonstrate the importance of continued training resulted in one well-known saying that the performance was *Afghan good enough*. Even though GERSOF offered multiple training opportunities, the PSU believed that proper repetitions were not necessary once they demonstrated competence in executing the operational task.

---

[221] Long et al., *Building Special Operations Partnerships*.

[222] Blakey, "A Formula for Trust."

[223] Doherty, "Letting Them Scrape a Knee: Advising for Third Order Effects."

In contrast to the ISAF, the RS mandate offered advisors fewer possibilities to train their counterparts in ways tailored to their condition. The limited personnel available to provide TAA to the Afghans changed the main effort of the training by primarily focusing on the key players. Nevertheless, certain Afghan security force capabilities were satisfactorily reported up the chain-of-command even when reality deemed such assessments an unsatisfactory truth. Most importantly, measuring the effectiveness of the training relies on observing the implementation of that training during operations. It is imperative that advisors have the opportunity for combat advising in order to assess the effort of the partner unit and therefore be able to adjust its training.

3.   Incentives

The German advisors needed to use certain incentives to motivate the PSU to train and operate in an effective way.[224] The main incentives, which the GERSOF could influence, were the reputation of the unit, the equipment and material provided, and the coalition assets available during combat operations. Apart from the extra pay from the Afghan MOI, the German advisors did not have the authority to dispense money in addition to the salary to influence the troopers of the PSU. The leadership of the PSU BLK, however, found several ways to make a profit to supplement their salaries, such as selling fuel and ammunition, which had "gone missing" during training and operations. The advisory teams had no assertive influence on who of their partner force should be promoted. On the other hand, filling PSU capability gaps with GERSOF supplies and assets motivated the unit to operate.

The reputation of the unit could be strengthened first through successful missions, especially when missions were carried out with other ANDSF units and when the PSU leadership was seen cooperating and working together with GERSOF. Furthermore, any operational success stories of the PSU needed to be reported not only to their respective chain-of-command of the GCPSU but, more impor-

---

[224] Hosek, *The Role of Incentive Pays in Military Compensation.*

tantly, to the PCOP.[225] Meetings with the PCOP were the most fruit-ful KLEs because the PCOP directed the payroll system and salaries for the PSU.[226] Those meetings were the most influential meetings for GERSOF to operationalize incentives to their advantage. As soon as the PCOP knew the strengths and weaknesses of the PSU, and thus how to use his security assets, he had the power to put pressure on them to conduct training and operations by approving additional support from the MOI for them. Numerous KLEs were possible under both NATO mandates, whereas under RS, only key leaders in BLK province could be engaged. Important leaders in rural areas or other provinces of northern Afghanistan were mainly out of reach.

Decreased combat advising between ISAF and RS resulted in fewer operational successes, which made it difficult for advisors to promote their success to the Afghan government and NATO in order to gain additional resources for enhancing their combat power and leveraging their unity of effort.[227] The relationship with the coalition forces, however, provided access to needed equipment and supplies. Unfortunately, from the perspective of the PSU, the main purpose of these additional supplies was not to improve the unit's skills during training or be more effective on the battlefield, but to gain additional profit. Nonetheless, without questioning an individual police officer about his true reason for combating Afghan's enemies, as long as the police officers fought, GERSOF used these incentives to train, equip, and conduct missions. With the decline of the coalition support under RS, incentives diminished as thriving factors for the PSU, and af-fected operational effectiveness and willingness to execute operations. This study claims that no additional support was needed from the international community, but going forward, what is available should be invested in a more efficient manner based on the experiences on the ground.

The access to coalition assets through the advisors during op-erations motivated the PSU to conduct more complex and high-risk

[225] Long et al., *Building Special Operations Partnerships*.

[226] Johnson and Zellen, *Culture, Conflict, and Counterinsurgency*.

[227] Lamb, "Perspectives on Emerging SOF Roles and Missions."

operations because they gained not only additional material and financial incentives, but also a certain sense of independence and additional security from this support. Under ISAF, more air assets for transportation and close air support (CAS) were available for the PSU through the advisors. Certain mission sets, especially time-sensitive targets, made it necessary to be quickly on the scene. With the coalition force assets, the Afghans could conduct missions that were otherwise not possible. As the AAF improved more and more during this time, however, they were less available due to competition with the higher prioritized national mission units. The access to CAS was decisive because these assets were only available through the SOF advisors on scene, which provided the PSU troopers a certain sense of security and invulnerability.[228] The advisors could assess the situation, whether CAS was needed or whether the PSU was capable to execute their mission on their own. The restriction under RS made fewer incentives available for the advisors to address the challenges of maintaining personnel and equipment readiness, responding to higher attrition, and combating fatigue of the PSU. This study claims that a minimum number of advisors assisting on the battlefield is necessary to know when the Afghan partner has to be motivated with additional assets to conduct their missions.

4.   Interaction among Factors

The interaction effects among the factors *constraints, training,* and *incentives* resulted in different outcomes and *relationships* between GERSOF and PSU BLK. Interaction effects exist when one factor's impact depends on the value of another factor. In this case, it turned out that the factor *constraints* had a significant impact on the factors *training* and *incentives,* whereas these factors *training* and *incentives* had no significant impact on the factor *constraints.* Toward the end of the ISAF mandate, the GERSOF's efforts to build trust and shape enduring *relationships* were already disadvantaged by the *constraints* of the time-based policy on training and reporting the progress of the part-

---

[228] Bruce R. Pirnie et al., *Beyond Close Air Support: Forging a New Air-Ground Partnership* (Santa Monica, CA: RAND Corporation, 2005), https://www.rand.org/pubs/monographs/MG301.html.

ner forces. With a fixed withdrawal date, advisors had to report the unit's progress toward independence against the advisors' own best knowledge. Even though the condition-based approach of the RS mandate was encouraging and aimed in the right direction, it further degraded the relationship between the GERSOF and PSU BLK. First, because the status of the unit had already been certified as independent, the Afghan will to train and cooperate was limited. Second, the advisors were constrained by having fewer mandatory assets, such as medical support, and fewer resources with which to motivate their partners.

The experience of the GERSOF and PSU working together demonstrated that the factor *training* mattered most when the factor *incentives* was present. When combat advising was still permitted under ISAF, the assets and skills of the GERSOF advisors were advantageous as *incentives*. With the shift from ISAF to RS, the advisors as well as their Afghan partners were aware that resources would be reduced. Therefore, fewer *incentives* were available for the advisors to stimulate Afghans who already demonstrated little motivation to train and fight. To meet the NATO policy objective for ending the combat role by 2014, GERSOF advisors were compelled to change the measures of progress. While some forces sought autonomy, others felt they were going to be abandoned. In contrast to RS, under ISAF advisors had a greater degree of freedom to train partner forces and to use *incentives*, but TAA were focused on time-based effects, and less on conditions.

The factor *training* had no impact on *constraints*, nor a major impact on *incentives*. The PSU BLK were not intrinsically motivated to train in a proper way; therefore, incentives were needed. For operational success in certain mission sets, especially in remote areas, the PSU lacked internal sustainment capabilities.[229] To extend their capability through lift assets, the PSU has depended heavily on coalition support. Going forward, the slowly progressing Afghan SMW can become capable of filling this gap unilaterally, but only in the distant future. Most important, with the shift towards non-combat TAA, the

---

[229] Department of Defense, *Enhancing Security and Stability in Afghanistan,* 105.

advisors were not allowed to witness the actual progress on the battle-field, which resulted in an overreliance on the Afghan reports about PSU's abilities. Certainly, the needed *training* and assistance at the higher levels of the PSU and up the hierarchal system also resulted in beneficial relationships for both sides, but they could not compensate for the assessment of GERSOF. Hence, the PSU could not serve as reliable intelligence sensors for GERSOF, and, in general, for the coalition forces. The tactical *constraints* and the associated resources available under RS made the GERSOF's efforts to motivate their partners to train and operate effectively dissatisfying.

D.   Conclusion

This study aims to recommend ways to use the resources, as-sets, and skills of SOF more effectively in shaping relationships with their partner force, tailoring these recommendations specifically to the Afghan circumstances related to national identity. This case study is neither about winning the war nor about significantly improving the performance of the ASSF, because solving the ongoing challenges in Afghanistan goes beyond the scope of this analysis. The ANDSF cannot maintain security today in Afghanistan and certainly will not be able to do so after the departure of U.S. and ally forces.[230] Hence, strong and reliable relationships can provide Western powers the op-portunity to engage indirectly with a small footprint and to back the government long enough either so that the adversary side comes to the negotiating table, or so that nation building can occur and the insurgencies become irrelevant.[231] This study aims to maintain the hard-won, but fragile, gains by the Afghans and the international community.

Despite all the aforementioned problems, combined joint training and combat experiences have led to the creation of numerous personal relationships between GERSOF and their partner units, and with other SOF allies. These relationships enabled to establish some bubbles of excellence. In contrast with the time-based approach in

---

[230] Mason, *The Strategic Lessons Unlearned*, vii-3.

[231] Liddell Hart, *Strategy: The Indirect Approach*.

previous strategies, this case study demonstrates that training and combat advising of Afghan forces can lead to enduring relationships when SOF advisors can provide TAA based on the condition of the partner unit. Furthermore, the insufficient quantity of SOF advisors can be addressed through fewer constraints and more autonomy for SOF in conducting tailored-to-mission MA, whereas the partner force's lack of motivation to train and operate can be countered through certain incentives, such as coalition assets and resources.

IV. THE FUTURE OF BUILDING ENDURING RELATIONSHIPS

Analysis of the factors of *constraints, training,* and *incentives* in the previous case studies demonstrated not only the opportunities but also the flaws of current NATO SOF approaches to build enduring *relationships.* NATO SOF are currently expanding their assistance to Afghan and Iraqi security forces to bolster their fights against insurgents and terror networks. Building strong relationships with their respective partners must remain a priority in NATO SOF's strategy and policy. NATO SOF and senior leaders, however, sometimes fail to identify and select the required priorities needed to allow the tactical SOF units to operate efficiently in different asymmetric environments by, with, and through indigenous partners. This failure to support and enable SOF elements to build enduring relationships will most likely continue to hamper Western strategy and policy goals while squandering valuable assets and resources.

In this chapter, the authors first discuss the case findings along with the associated factors and, second, identify the recommendations for SOF senior leaders as well as opportunities for researchers to test the findings. The analysis suggests that current SOF approaches to building enduring relationships with their counterparts in fragile or failed states can be made more effective by slightly adjusting the interaction among the studied factors of *constraints, training,* and *incentives.* It is understood that political goals and national strategic objectives define the framework for *constraints.* In most cases, SOF have to accept and operate under those specified constraints, but SOF are able to influence the factors of *training* and *incentives.* Both factors significantly matter especially when the factor of *constraints* is present. SOF's ability to influence these two factors determines how powerful the relationship with SOF partners is going to be, as well as the degree to which that relationship can enhance operational effectiveness.

A. Findings

After the Cold War, Western interventions primarily focused on security assistance operations, ranging from ensuring humanitarian aid delivery to launching the GWOT after 9/11. The focus of these assistance efforts was building partner capacity, but their outcomes often failed to meet the expectations of Western powers. Major setbacks, such as the collapse of the Iraqi army facing ISIS in 2014 and the short occupation of Kunduz city by the Taliban in 2015, challenged the sustainability of yearlong training efforts and the ability of the partner forces to operate independently, especially when executing missions without NATO SOF combat advisors.[232] Inevitably, such examples raise the question of how NATO states can maintain the established efforts and relations in order to secure areas of fragile or failed states over an even longer period.[233] This remains a challenge for NATO SOF organizations, in particular, when the majority of coalition forces have left the conflict zone and the social-political support of the Western states has diminished. This thesis claims that as long as the host nation's will meets the Western objectives to remain engaged, then both sides should have the ability to preserve situational awareness and to reduce the risk of significant shortcomings.

Post 9/11, the NATO efforts have severely lacked institutional strength in engaging asymmetric conflicts. The NATO SOF members mainly reflect their own image and expectations, which were created by the experiences of the last century. Unfortunately, the partner forces in fragile and weak states are often not capable of advancing at the desired pace of Western decision makers.[234] Even when the known approaches do not effectively strengthen long-term relations between SOF and partner forces, due to the interaction of institutional, social, and political dynamics, Western leadership continues to apply flawed strategies, intensifying threats on the ground. Perhaps their very nature as large, bureaucratic institutions makes NATO

---

[232] Goldstein and Mashal, "Taliban Fighters Capture Kunduz City."

[233] Karlin, *Building Militaries in Fragile States.*

[234] Karlin.

states ill suited for asymmetric conflicts.[235] Thus, when NATO SOF' performance expectations, in contrast to the partner force expectations, create a gap, the NATO states' response is usually to fill the gap by sending more troops, spending more money, and providing more equipment and resources instead of adjusting the purpose and ends of the engagements based on past lessons, best practices, and strategic theories.

The nature of social and political dynamics in Western states seems to be the root of shortcomings in Afghanistan that have not been adequately addressed, leading to similar follow-on failings in Iraq and Syria. The authors claim that needed changes in strategy will not occur due to the low threat of asymmetric wars to Western states, which results in less commitment from policy makers to reform. NATO SOF operators, on the other hand, working at the tactical level are intrinsically motivated and dedicated to their mission because they have to face the direct consequences of their actions.[236] Hence, at least the tactics within the flawed strategies have to be adjusted from the bottom up, along the lines of the analyzed factors in this study.

The authors offer the argument that current NATO SOF approaches to building enduring relationships with their counterparts in fragile or failed states can be made more effective by adjusting the interaction of the factors *constraints, training,* and *incentives.* Based on the findings of the case studies, this analysis suggests that applying tactical and local realities into new TTPs for SOF advisors in asymmetric conflicts will more likely lead to enduring relationships, which are more appropriate to the Western (geo)political objectives in these conflict zones. Within the prevailing constraints, the NATO SOF advisors repeatedly attempted—with varying outcomes—to motivate and operationalize their partner forces to meet Western expectations through training and incentives. In both cases analyzed in this study, NATO SOF units deployed to provide TAA to their counterparts and

---

[235] Ben Barry, *Harsh Lessons: Iraq, Afghanistan and the Changing Character of War* (Abingdon: Routledge, 2017).
[236] Barry.

conduct combined joint operations against insurgent groups. The attempt to build enduring relationships was implemented in different ways according to the prevailing *constraints*, *training* purposes, and the *incentives* available to each unit.

The military bureaucracies imposing the constraints do not provide the adequate flexibility to apply varying SOF approaches tailored to the fluctuating circumstances. Introducing time-based constraints along with Western expectations or limiting the AO for SOF units, as this study demonstrated, creates challenges where the national identity and loyalty of a diverse population vary broadly. Due to complex, time-sensitive, and challenging operational environments, SOF units are sometimes forced to operate in a gray zone between what is legally permitted and lawfully prohibited without guidance from senior leaders.[237] SOF, as Thomas K. Adams argues, are "a unique politico-military instrument, capable of operating in the vague gray area between political conflict and open war."[238]

Ill-suited training and undefined operational objectives can occasionally transform into a net-negative for both sides: the SOF advisors, who want to meet the expectations of their superiors, and the partner force that is neither willing nor capable to deliver these demands. This creates a gap and most likely leads to disappointments that can be counterproductive in establishing trust and respect for enduring relationships. In the hope of overcoming such gaps, SOF advisors often resort to the use of incentives, which have risks and benefits. Incentives are necessary to encourage and direct the partner forces in a proper manner, but incentives carry a certain degree of acknowledged dependency.[239]

The misuse or over-reliance on incentives can lead to contrary effects. Even with the assumption that the partner force will collapse without external support, the use of incentives through training and

---

[237] Votel et al., "Unconventional Warfare in the Gray Zone," 108–109.

[238] Thomas K. Adams, *U.S. Special Operations Forces in Action: The Challenge of Unconventional Warfare* (New York: Psychological Press, 1998), 11.

[239] Charles Michael Johnson, *Security Force Assistance: DoD's Consideration of Unintended Consequences, Perverse Incentives, and Moral Hazards,* GAO 13-241R (Washington, DC: Government Accountability Office, 2013), 1–2.

operations should allow the partner forces to be capable of conducting certain operations absent any SOF advisory support. Whereas accompanied, advised, and assisted operations with immediate effects should be limited to main areas and in-extremis cases. This demands a certain degree of leading by perception for the advisors to choose the best-suited incentives in a minimum needed amount.

Healthy, sustainable relationships can arise if political/strategic decision makers of the partner nation and NATO states focus on patience and long-term progress rather than on short-term fixes mainly aimed at meeting domestic political demands.

B.   Recommendations

Based on analysis of the case studies, the authors derived the following recommendations to prevent countries from (again) becoming international terrorist safe-havens. The authors assume that these recommended actions will not require more troops nor will it cost significantly more than the current expenses of the applied strategy. The recommendations are not about winning asymmetric wars nor significantly improving the performance of the partner forces. Only a change in strategy—not tactics—can resolve the strategic nature of these conflicts. Hence, the recommendations primarily aim to improve the tactics of SOF advisors by using the existing SOF resources and personnel more effectively, tailored to the current circumstances of the partner forces confronting their opponents.

Before these recommendations can be implemented, the authors acknowledge that these findings have to be tested against a broader range of SOF interactions with partner forces in the post-9/11 era. In cases with similar constraints and training purposes, SOF capabilities should able to be explained by the theory. Additionally, the attempts of other NATO members or other agencies, such as intelligence agencies, could provide substance to the theory. Further insights into effective means of maintaining relations over time could be gained through the approaches of non-Western states, such as Iran successfully supporting Hamas and Hezbollah for decades, or Iran throughout the 1990s when that state "had been the primary sponsor of the Northern Alliance, a group of anti-Taliban forces."[240]

In the Iraq case, the factor that holds the most promise for improvement is *training*, specifically in DANSOF's ability to stimulate the AFB's self-motivation. As this study showed, DANSOF were able to enhance the AFB's morale, confidence, and their esprit de corps through training. The AFB learned how to plan and execute missions independently and to operate without relying primarily on external support. DANSOF proved that working by, with, and through the AFB, DANSOF enhanced not only the AFB's capacity to fight ISIS, but also aligned the Sunni-multitribe organization in western Al Anbar with the Shia-led central government of Iraq. DANSOF's strong relationship with the AFB enabled them to achieve operational success. By contrast, many other NATO SOF organizations only marginally improved the efficiency of local forces, but simultaneously misaligned local interests and inadvertently contributed to corruption, which contributed to the destabilization of the unit's respective AO.[241] DANSOF flawlessly demonstrated that a 'small footprint' approach with the right combination of *constraints, training,* and *incentives* could enable them to build and maintain relatively strong and genuine relationships with the AFB through persistent and culturally attuned engagements. They effectively engaged with Iraqi Sunni tribal leaders, with principals of the Shia parliament, and with other NATO SOF members, pursuing very clear objectives shared between trainers and trained, creating a natural exit strategy for NATO forces. This may illustrate a simple but effective MA model that yields improved results, based on the understanding that the 'small footprint' approach is likely the only available choice in the Middle East due to the change in Western security priorities toward near-peer conventional threats and the lack of results from the two-large interventions in Afghanistan and

---

[240] Trita Parsi, *Treacherous Alliance: The Secret Dealings of Israel, Iran, and the United States* (New Haven, CT: Yale University Press, 2008), 226.

[241] Stephen Biddle, Julia Macdonald, and Ryan Baker, "Small Footprint, Small Payoff: The Military Effectiveness of Security Force Assistance," *Journal of Strategic Studies* 41, no. 1-2 (2018): 90–94, https://doi.org/10.1080/01402390.2017.1307745.

Iraq. Moreover, the training of a Sunni-militia in Shia-dominated Iraq highlights many of the political dilemmas and pitfalls that occur when SOF operate in highly fractured societies.

Incentives played a vital role in this case study; however, for the AFB incentives were more than just monetary-induced motivation. The factor *incentives* went beyond financial reimbursement because the AFB was intrinsically motivated to liberate occupied tribal territory and rescue family members. The AFB acknowledged DANSOF's true partnership and intentions to train, advise, assist, and accompany them as the most valuable *incentive* the tribes could have ever obtained. In turn, DANSOF recognized that tribes will always play a vital role as a social institution in the Middle East. Tribes are essential for any successful strategy against ISIS. Tribes must be included in any effort to provide security and stability in those rural communities. They often can provide essential connections within their local community institutions and point out the key players in the provincial and central governments. The SOF's ability to build and maintain relationships with tribes will determine how strong the partnership is going to be, either enhancing or diminishing the chances of future operational success. Operationalizing the tribes and enabling them to operate on their own—diplomatically, informationally, militarily, economically, and politically—will provide strategic opportunities.[242] These opportunities require strong partnerships to ensure those efforts are nested within the overall strategic objectives.

In the Afghanistan case, the factor that holds the most promise for improvement is *constraints*, particularly in a condition-based approach rather than a time-based one. This will allow the advisory teams to adjust their training and ratio on missions according to the capacity of their partner unit. Advisors in COIN need to be invested in reaching and maintaining certain partner capabilities so partner forces can stand on their own and know when to take the lead. If local forces are the long-term solution to security, advisors must have the possibility to provide TAA tailored to the mindset,

---

[242] Robert D. Blackwill and Jennifer M. Harris, *War by Other Means: Geoeconomics and Statecraft* (Cambridge, MA: Harvard University Press, 2017).

motivation, and skills of the partner force. Like any Western SOF unit, each partner unit has its strengths and weaknesses. Some have already reached certain levels, and others are on their way. The performance of the partner units mainly depends on the units' superiors and leadership to support, train, and use their unit members properly; the unit's will and motivation to fight; the security situation of each AO; and, foremost, whether the unit is partnered with and therefore has access to assets and skills of coalition forces to fight external supported adversaries.

Therefore, with the assumption of no additional SOF units, the golden-hour *constraint* has to be extended by giving the SOF medics/paramedics more responsibilities in treating casualties, or by providing more SOST along with advisors to foster the effectiveness of their partner units across the country. Then, the advisors will no longer be limited, can reach out to hotspots, and can support units that are no longer partnered or supply new units where they are desperately needed. Even if the advising would not be constant, more unsecured area could be covered if the advisors could focus on assisting greater combined missions to bolster the effectiveness of partner forces along with the conventional forces, whenever the enemy situation demands it. A less effective, but easier to implement, option would be for the partner units that are not partnered or no longer reachable by the advisors due to mandate limitations to get the opportunity for small unit exchanges. For example, the former German-partnered PSUs in KDZ and BGL province could get the training and skills in the area of Mazar-e Sharif on a regular basis to maintain those relationships, and they could extend training levels in order to understand the situation in the areas without coalition forces. The Afghan units themselves will have the opportunity to share their experiences among them.

Moreover, the creation of coalition SOF advisory teams would enhance individual military skills and the range of movement. As the *constraints* factor illustrated in the DANSOF and SEAL cases, the different multinational SOF units operate under different mandates with their own national caveats, which results in different ROEs. This leads to situations in which two units from different nations operate on the same battlefield under different constraints, allowing them to compensate for one another's gaps by having access to more assets, equipment, and shared intelligence. These multinational SOF advisor teams could integrate their teams if they are tailored to their individual capabilities and constraints in order to gain synergetic effects on the battlefield. Increased interoperability between military institutions and civilian agencies through partnership will also benefit combined planning and operational efforts.

Overall, SOF can strengthen the bonds among the *constraints, training,* and *incentives* factors to establish strong *relationships.* A key component of strong relationships is the integration of foreign partners into combined operations. Leveraging a partnership requires persistent engagement. One cannot simply "surge" trust. A small-scale, low-visibility SOF element can achieve strategic success through enduring relationships, which are crucial for leading the indirect strategy in current and future conflicts. Further, these enduring links between partners can provide experience and intelligence sharing within the partner nation, within the NATO alliance, or more broadly, throughout the international community. Relationships empower SOF to perform as a highly skilled and reliable cadre in collaboration with local partner forces to prevent and solve shared problems, sometimes accomplishing more with less.

About the authors:

Torsten Gojowsky is a U.S. Army Special Forces Officer with several deployments to the Middle East, Europe, and Southeast Asia. He earned his Master of Science degree in Defense Analysis with a specialty track of Irregular Warfare from the Naval Postgraduate School and currently holds a position at the U.S. Army John F. Kennedy Special Warfare Center and School.

Sebastian Koegler is a German Army Officer with several deployments to Afghanistan. He earned his Master of Science degree in Defense Analysis with a specialty track of Irregular Warfare from the Naval Postgraduate School.

LIST OF REFERENCES

Adams, Thomas K. *U.S. Special Operations Forces in Action: The Challenge of Unconventional Warfare.* New York: Psychological Press, 1998.

Al Bawaba. "At Least 25% of Al-Qaim in Iraq 'Totally Destroyed' after ISIS." November 16, 2017. https://www.albawaba.com/behind-news/least-25-al-qaim-iraq-totally-destroyed-after-isis-1049060.

Aljazeera. "ISIL Loses Al-Qaim in Iraq and Deir Az Zor in Syria." November 3, 2017. https://www.aljazeera.com/news/2017/11/isil-loses-al-qaim-iraq-deir-az-zor-syria-171103185913263.html.

Altman, George R., and Leo Shane. "The Obama Era Is Over. Here's How the Military Rates His Legacy." *Military Times,* August 8, 2017. https://www.militarytimes. com/news/2017/01/08/the-obama-era-is-over-here-s-how-the-military-rates-his-legacy/.

Alvarez, John, Robert Nalepa, Anna-Marie Wyant, and Fred Zimmerman. *Special Operations Forces Reference Manual.* Tampa, FL: Joint Special Operations University, 2015.

Amble, John, and Liam Collins. "How New Is the New Afghanistan Strategy?." Modern War Institute. August 21, 2017. https://mwi.usma.edu/new-new-afghanistan-strategy/.

Anderson, Joel. "Provincial Response Companies Train for Special Missions." DVIDS. March 29, 2013. https://www.dvidshub.net/news/106023/provincial-response-companies-train-special-missions.

Arreguín-Toft, Ivan. "How the Weak Win Wars: A Theory of Asymmetric Conflict." *International Security* 26, no. 1, (2001): 93–128.

Bapat, Navin A. "State Bargaining with Transnational Terrorist Groups." *International Studies Quarterly* 50, no. 1 (March 2006): 213–229.

Barry, Ben. *Harsh Lessons: Iraq, Afghanistan and the Changing Character of War.* Abingdon, UK: Routledge, 2017.

Basquez, Andrew. "SF Returns to Its Roots with 4th Battalion Redesign." *Special Warfare* 26, no. 4 (October 2013): 9–10.

Beach, Derek, and Rasmus Brun Pedersen. *Process-Tracing Methods: Foundations and Guidelines.* Ann Arbor: University of Michigan Press, 2013.

Behr, Timo. "Germany and Regional Command-North: ISAF's Weakest Link?." In *Statebuilding in Afghanistan: Multinational Contributions to Reconstruction,* edited by Nik Hynek and Péter Marton, 42–64. New York: Routledge, 2011.

Bengali, Shashank. "These Are Afghanistan's Best Troops. The U.S. Is Backing a Plan to Create Many More of Them." *Los Angeles Times,* December 9, 2017. http://www. latimes.com/world/asia/la-fg-afghanistan-special-operations-20171209-htmlstory.html.

Benraad, Myriam. "Iraq's Tribal 'Sahwa': Its Rise and Fall." *Middle East Policy* 18, no. 1 (January 2011): 121–131. https://doi.org/10.1111/j.1475-4967.2011.00477.

Bergen, Peter. *The Longest War: The Enduring Conflict between America and Al-Qaeda.* New York: Free Press, 2011.

Biddle, Stephen, Julia Macdonald, and Ryan Baker. "Small Footprint, Small Payoff: The Military Effectiveness of Security Force Assistance." *Journal of Strategic Studies* 41, no. 1–2 (2018): 89–142. https://doi.org/10.1080/01402390.2017.1307745.

Binnendijk, Hans. *Friends, Foes, and Future Directions: U.S. Partnerships in a Turbulent World.* Santa Monica, CA: RAND Corporation, 2016.

Bitzinger, Richard. *Denmark, Norway, and NATO: Constraints and Challenges.* Santa Monica, CA: RAND Corporation, 1989.

Blackwill, Robert D., and Jennifer M. Harris. *War by Other Means: Geoeconomics and Statecraft.* Cambridge, MA: Harvard University Press, 2017.

Blakey, John. "A Formula for Trust." Management-Issues. April 27, 2016. https://www. management-issues.com/opinion/7171/a-formula-for-trust/.

Blanken, Leo J., Hy S. Rothstein, and Jason J. Lepore, eds. *Assessing War: The Challenge of Measuring Success and Failure.* Washington, DC: Georgetown University Press, 2015.

Bosiljevac, T. L. *SEALs: UDT/SEAL Operations in Vietnam.* Boulder, CO: Paladin Press, 1990.

Brown, Seyom. "Purposes and Pitfalls of War by Proxy: A Systemic Analysis." *Small Wars & Insurgencies* 27, no. 2 (2016): 243–257.

Builta, Jeffrey A., and Eric N. Heller. "Reflections on 10 Years of Counterterrorism Analysis." *Studies in Intelligence* 55, no. 3 (2011): 1–15.

Burton, Janice. "SWCS to Dedicate Kennedy-Yarborough Statue." United States Army. March 28, 2012. https://www.army.mil/article/76701/swcs_to_dedicate_kennedy_yarborough_statue.

Byman, Daniel. "Outside Support for Insurgent Movements." *Studies in Conflict & Terrorism* 36, no. 12 (2013): 981–1004.

Campbell, John. *International Trauma Life Support for Emergency Care Providers.* London: Pearson Education, 2013.

Chivers, C. J. "War without End." *New York Times,* August 8, 2018. https://www. nytimes.com/2018/08/08/magazine/war-afghanistan-iraq-soldiers.html.

Christia, Fotini. *Alliance Formation in Civil Wars.* Cambridge: Cambridge University Press, 2012.

Clausewitz, Carl von. *On War.* Translated by Michael Howard and Peter Paret. Princeton, NJ: Princeton University Press, 1989.

Cleveland, Charles. "ARSOF 2022—PART II: Changing the Institution U.S. Army Special Operations Command." *Special Warfare* 27, no. 3 (July 2014): 3–9.

———. "Special Operations Theory Symposium Remarks 30 August 2016." *Special Operations Theory* 3, JSOU Report 17–6. Tampa, FL: Joint Special Operations University Press, 2017, 11–24.

CNN. "Operation Iraqi Freedom and Operation New Dawn Fast Facts." Accessed November 21, 2017. http://www.cnn.com/2013/10/30/world/meast/operation-iraqi-freedom-and-operation-new-dawn-fast-facts/index.html.

————. "September 11th Terror Attacks Fast Facts." Accessed November 21, 2017. http://www.cnn.com/2013/07/27/us/september-11-anniversary-fast-facts/index.html.

Coll, Steve. *Directorate S: The C.I.A. and America's Secret Wars in Afghanistan and Pakistan.* New York: Penguin Books, 2018.

————. *Ghost Wars: The Secret History of the CIA, Afghanistan, and Bin Laden, from the Soviet Invasion to September 10, 2001.* New York: Penguin Books, 2004.

Cook, John L. *Afghanistan: The Perfect Failure.* Bloomington, IN: Xlibris Corporation, 2012.

Cooper, Helene, and Matthew Rosenberg. "After Gains against ISIS, Pentagon Focuses on Mosul." *New York Times,* February 29, 2016. https://www.nytimes.com/2016/03/01/world/middleeast/after-gains-against-isis-american-focus-is-turning-to-mosul.html.

Cordesman, Anthony H. "U.S. Wars in Iraq, Syria, Libya and Yemen: What Are the End States?." CSIS. August 15, 2016. https://www.csis.org/analysis/us-wars-iraq-syria-libya-and-yemen-what-are-endstates.

Cumming-Bruce, Nick. "ISIS Committed Genocide against Yazidis in Syria and Iraq, U.N. Panel Says." *New York Times,* June 16, 2016. https://www.nytimes.com/2016/06/17/world/middleeast/isis-genocide-yazidi-un.html.

Davis, Daniel L. "Truth, Lies, and Afghanistan." *Armed Forces Journal,* February 1, 2012. http://armedforcesjournal.com/truth-lies-and-afghanistan/.

Dearden, Lizzie. "Almost 10,000 Yazidis 'Killed or Kidnapped in Isis Genocide but True Scale of Horror May Never Be Known.'" *Independent,* May 9, 2017. https://www.independent.co.uk/news/world/middle-east/isis-islamic-state-yazidi-sex-slaves-genocide-sinjar-death-toll-number-kidnapped-study-un-lse-a7726991.html.

Defense News. "Denmark to Reinforce Military Fight against ISIS." April 21, 2016. https://www.defensenews.com/global/2016/04/21/denmark-to-reinforce-military-fight-against-isis/.

Department of Defense. *Enhancing Security and Stability in Afghanistan.* Washington, DC: Government Printing Office, December 15, 2017. https://www.defense.gov/News/News-Releases/ News-Release-View/Article/1397079/dod-releases-report-on-enhancing-security-and-stability-in-afghanistan/.

———. "Operation Inherent Resolve." Accessed May 23, 2018. http://www. inherentresolve.mil/.

Department of the Army. *U.S. Army Counterinsurgency,* FM 3–24. Washington, DC: Department of the Army, 2006. https://www.hsdl.org/?abstract &did=468442.

Doherty, Thomas. "Letting Them Scrape a Knee: Advising for Third Order Effects." *Small Wars Journal,* accessed May 3, 2018. http://smallwarsjournal.com/jrnl/art/letting-them-scrape-a-knee-advising-for-third-order-effects#i2.

Dominguez, Gabriel. "ANDSF Failing to Extend Control over Afghan Districts, Says SIGAR." Jane's 360. July 31, 2018. https://www.janes.com/article/82111/andsf-failing-to-extend-control-over-afghan-districts-says-sigar.

Facebook. "A'ali Al-Furat Facebook Page." Accessed May 20, 2018. https://www. facebook.com/furatupper.80/.

Fairweather, Jack. *The Good War: Why We Couldn't Win the War or the Peace in Afghanistan.* New York: Basic Books, 2014.

Farrell, Theo, Frans P. B. Osinga, and James A. Russell, eds. *Military Adaptation in Afghanistan.* Stanford, CA: Stanford University Press, 2013.

Feilke, Markus. "German Experiences in Police Building in Afghanistan." GRIPS Policy Research Center, no. 10–02 (January 2010): 1–26. http://www.grips.ac.jp/r-center/wp-content/ uploads/10-02.pdf.

Fischer, John. "Humanitarian Law in the Fight against ISIS." United States Central Command. March 14, 2017. http://www.centcom.mil/MEDIA/NEWS-ARTICLES/ News-Article-View/Article/1111935/humanitarian-law-in-the-fight-against-isis/.

Fitzgerald, David. *Learning to Forget: U.S. Army Counterinsurgency Doctrine and Practice from Vietnam to Iraq.* Stanford, CA: Stanford University Press, 2013.

Forsvaret. "Jægerkorpsets Historie." [History of the Danish Army SOF] Accessed May 20, 2018. http://forsvaret.dk/JGK/Om%20J%C3%A6gerkorpset/Historie/Pages/default.aspx.

Fort Campbell Courier. "SF Expansion Begins with Fort Campbell's 5th Group." August 14, 2008. http://fortcampbellcourier.com/news/article_075ef8cf-b7f2-5bc5-9044-4d87a2133228.html.

Friend, Alice Hunt. "The Accompany They Keep: What Niger Tells Us about Accompany Missions, Combat, and Operations Other than War." War on the Rocks. May 11, 2018. https://warontherocks.com/2018/05/the-accompany-they-keep-what-niger-tells-us-about-accompany-missions-combat-and-operations-other-than-war/.

George, Alexander L., and Andrew Bennett. *Case Studies and Theory Development in the Social Sciences.* Cambridge, MA: MIT Press, 2005.

Georges, Jayson. "Honor and Shame Societies: 9 Keys to Working with Muslims." Zwemer Center. Accessed August 7, 2018. http://www.zwemercenter.com/guide/honor-and-shame-9-keys/.

German Federal Parliament. "Bundestagsdrucksache 15/5996." [German Federal Parliament Printed Document] September 21, 2005. http//dip21.bundestag.de/dip21/btd/15/059/1505996.pdf.

————. "Deutscher Bundestag—Resolute Support Mission." Accessed May 2, 2018. https://www.bundestag.de/ausschuesse/ausschuesse18/a12/auslandseinsaetze/auslandseinsaetze/rsm/363988.

Gibbons-Neff, Thomas, and Dan Lamothe. "Obama Administration Expands Elite Military Unit's Powers to Hunt Foreign Fighters Globally." *Washington Post,* November 25, 2016. https://www.washingtonpost.com/news/checkpoint/wp/2016/11/25/obama-administration-expands-elite-military-units-powers-to-hunt-foreign-fighters-globally/?utm_term=.e899ae59773a.

Giustozzi, Antonio. "Auxiliary Irregular Forces in Afghanistan: 1978–2008." In *Making Sense of Proxy Wars: States, Surrogates & the Use of Force,* edited by William Banks, 89–107. Lincoln, NE: Potomac Books, 2012.

Glenn, Cameron. "Timeline: The Rise, Spread and Fall of the Islamic State." Wilson Center. July 5, 2016. https://www.wilsoncenter.org/article/timeline-the-rise-spread-and-fall-the-islamic-state.

Goldstein, Joseph, and Mujib Mashal. "Taliban Fighters Capture Kunduz City as Afghan Forces Retreat." *New York Times,* September 29, 2015. https://www.nytimes.com/2015/09/29/world/asia/taliban-fighters-enter-city-of-kunduz-in-northern-afghanistan.html.

Gonzalez, Roberto J. "On 'Tribes' and Bribes: 'Iraq Tribal Study,' Al-Anbar's Awakening, and Social Science." *Focaal* 53 (2009): 105–116. https://doi.org/10.3167/fcl.2009.530107.

Gould, Joe. "DoD's $1.8B Train-and-Equip Request Forecasts Chaos after ISIS." *Defense News*, June 1, 2017. https://www.defensenews.com/congress/budget/2017/06/01/dod-s-1-8b-train-and-equip-request-forecasts-chaos-after-isis/.

Grandpre, Andrew. "Inside Mosul, U.S. Military Advisers Wear Black to Blend in with Elite Iraqi Units." *Military Times,* March 26, 2017. https://www.militarytimes. com/news/your-military/2017/03/26/inside-mosul-u-s-military-advisers-wear-black-to-blend-in-with-elite-iraqi-units/.

Gronholt-Pedersen, Jacob. "Denmark Says Deploying Special Forces to Syria against Islamic State." Reuters. January 2, 2017. https://www.reuters.com/article/us-mideast-crisis-denmark/denmark-says-deploying-special-forces-to-syria-against-islamic-state-idUSKBN1541RA.

Guerin, Orla. "Iraq: Sunni Tribe 'Left for Slaughter' by Islamic State." BBC News. November 10, 2014. http://www.bbc.com/news/world-middle-east-29984668.

Helmus, Todd C. *Advising the Command: Best Practices from the Special Operation's Advisory Experience in Afghanistan.* Santa Monica, CA: RAND Corporation, 2015.

History. "U.S.-Led Attack on Afghanistan Begins—Oct 07, 2001."Accessed November 21, 2017. http://www.history.com/this-day-in-history/u-s-led-attack-on-afghanistan-begins.

Homiak, Travis. "A Blueprint for What Is Possible: The Value in a Theory of Special Warfare." *Special Operations Theory* 3, JSOU Report 17–6. Tampa, FL: Joint Special Operations University Press, 2017, 75–88.

Hosek, James. *The Role of Incentive Pays in Military Compensation.* Santa Monica, CA: RAND Corporation, 2010.

Irwin, Will. *The Jedburghs: The Secret History of the Allied Special Forces, France, 1944.* New York: Public Affairs, 2009.

Johnson, Charles Michael. *Security Force Assistance: DoD's Consideration of Unintended Consequences, Perverse Incentives, and Moral Hazards.* GAO 13–241R. Washington, DC: Government Accountability Office, 2013.

Johnson, Thomas H., and Barry Scott Zellen, eds. *Culture, Conflict, and Counterinsurgency.* Stanford, CA: Stanford University Press, 2014.

Johnson, Thomas H., and M. Chris Mason. "All Counterinsurgency Is Local." *The Atlantic,* October 2008. https://www.theatlantic.com/magazine/archive/2008/10/all-counterinsurgency-is-local/306965/.

Johnson, Thomas H., and Wali Shaaker. *Taliban Narratives: The Use and Power of Stories in the Afghanistan Conflict.* Oxford, UK: Oxford University Press, 2018.

Karlin, Mara E. *Building Militaries in Fragile States: Challenges for the United States.* Philadelphia: University of Pennsylvania Press, 2018.

Kime, Patricia. "'Golden Hour' Policy Saved U.S. Lives in Afghanistan." Armed Services Blood Program. October 5, 2015. http://www.militaryblood.dod.mil/ViewContent.aspx?con_id_pk=1968&fr=hs.

Kirkbride, Alec. *The Awakening: Arab Campaign, 1917–1918.* London: University Press of Arabia, 1971.

Lamb, Christopher. "Perspectives on Emerging SOF Roles and Missions." *Special Warfare* 8, no. 3 (July 1995): 2–9.

Liddell Hart, Basil H. *Strategy: The Indirect Approach.* New Delhi: Pentagon Press, 2012.

Locke, Edwin A. *Handbook of Principles of Organizational Behavior: Indispensable Knowledge for Evidence-Based Management.* Hoboken, NJ: John Wiley & Sons, 2009.

Long, Austin. "The Limits of Special Operations Forces." *PRISM* 6, no. 3 (December 7, 2016): 1–4. http://cco.ndu.edu/News/Article/1020184/the-limits-of-special-operations-forces/.

Long, Austin, Todd C. Helmus, Rebecca Zimmerman, Christopher M. Schnaubelt, and Peter Chalk. *Building Special Operations Partnerships in Afghanistan and Beyond: Challenges and Best Practices from Afghanistan, Iraq, and Colombia.* Santa Monica, CA: RAND Corporation, 2015.

Mack, Andrew. "Why Big Nations Lose Small Wars." *World Politics: A Quarterly Journal of International Relations* 27, no. 2 (1975): 175–200. https://doi.org/10.2307/2009880.

Maisel, Adam. "The Adviser's Dilemma: Endemic Challenges and Unrealized Opportunities in the Training Mission in Afghanistan." *Small Wars Journal* (blog), May 17, 2015. http://smallwarsjournal.com/blog/the-advisers-dilemma-endemic-challenges-and-unrealized-opportunities-in-the-training-mission-in.

Mason, M. Chris. *The Strategic Lessons Unlearned from Vietnam, Iraq, and Afghanistan: Why the Afghan National Security Forces Will Not Hold, and the Implications for the U.S. Army in Afghanistan.* Carlisle, PA: Strategic Studies Institute, 2015.

McChrystal, Stanley A. *Team of Teams: The Power of Small Groups in a Fragmented World.* New York: Penguin Books, 2015.

McInnis, Kathleen J., and Nathan J. Lucas. *What Is "Building Partner Capacity?" Issues for Congress.* CRS Report No. R44313. Washington, DC: Congressional Research Service, 2015. https://fas.org/sgp/crs/natsec/R44313.pdf.

McIntyre, Jamie, and Travis J. Tritten. "Jim Mattis Breaks down the New Afghanistan Strategy: The Goal, the Plan, What's Different and How It All Ends." *Washington Examiner,* October 4, 2017. https://www.washingtonexaminer.com/jim-mattis-breaks-down-the-new-afghanistan-strategy-the-goal-the-plan-whats-different-and-how-it-all-ends.

McLeary, Paul, and Lara Jakes. "U.S. Works to Bring More Sunni Tribal Fighters into Islamic State War." *Foreign Policy,* June 10, 2015. https://foreignpolicy.com/2015/06/10/more-u-s-advisers-in-iraq-to-train-sunni-tribes/.

McRaven, William H. *Spec Ops: Case Studies in Special Operations Warfare: Theory and Practice.* New York: Ballantine Books, 1996.

Miller, Aaron Davis. "Barack Obama's Play-It-Safe Approach." CNN. June 27, 2013. https://www.cnn.com/2013/06/27/opinion/miller-obama-risk-averse/index.html.

Montgomery, Gary W., and Timothy S. McWilliams, eds. *Al-Anbar Awakening: Iraqi Perspectives Vol. II.* Quantico, VA: Marine Corps University Press, 2009.

Mosul Study Group. *What the Battle for Mosul Teaches the Force.* 24th ed. United States Army Training and Doctrine Command, 2017. https://www.armyupress.army.mil/Portals/7/Primer-on-Urban-Operation/Documents/Mosul-Public-Release1.pdf.

Naffsinger, Peter A. "'Face' Among the Arabs." Central Intelligence Agency. September 18, 1995. https://www.cia.gov/library/center-for-the-study-of-intelligence/kent-csi/vol8no3/html/v08i3a05p_0001.htm.

Nakamura, David, and Abby Philip. "Trump Announces New Strategy for Afghanistan That Calls for a Troop Increase." *Washington Post,* August 21, 2017. https://www.washingtonpost.com/politics/trump-expected-to-announce-small-troop-increase-in-afghanistan-in-prime-time-address/2017/08/21/eb3a513e-868a-11e7-a94f-3139abce39f5_story.html?noredirect=on&utm_term=.aeaf0d e95b29.

Naylor, Seán D. "The Pentagon Ups the Ante in Syria Fight." *Foreign Policy,* March 30, 2015. https://foreignpolicy.com/2015/03/30/the-pentagon-ups-the-ante-in-syria-fight-iraq-islamic-state-delta-force/.

North Atlantic Treaty Organization. "ISAF's Mission in Afghanistan (2001–2014)." September 1, 2015. http://www.nato.int/cps/en/natohq/topics_69366.htm.

———. "NATO and Afghanistan." September 14, 2018. http://www.nato.int/cps/en/natohq/topics_8189.htm.

———. "Relations with Iraq." July 31, 2018. http://www.nato.int/cps/en/natohq/topics_88247.htm.

———. "Resolute Support Mission in Afghanistan." July 18, 2018. http://www.nato.int/cps/en/natohq/topics_113694.htm.

Noetzel, Timo. "The German Politics of War: Kunduz and the War in Afghanistan." *International Affairs* 87, no. 2 (2011): 397–417. https://doi.org/10.1111/j.1468-2346.2011.00979.x.

Noetzel, Timo, and Benjamin Schreer. *Spezialkräfte der Bundeswehr.* [Special Forces of the German armed forces] Berlin: Stiftung Wissenschaft und Politik, 2006.

Parsi, Trita. *Treacherous Alliance: The Secret Dealings of Israel, Iran, and the United States.* New Haven, CT: Yale University Press, 2008.

Pirnie, Bruce R., Alan J. Vick, Adam R. Grissom, Karl P. Mueller, and David T. Orletsky. *Beyond Close Air Support: Forging a New Air-*

Ground Partnership. Santa Monica, CA: RAND Corporation, 2005. https://www.rand.org/pubs/monographs/MG301.html.

Plaster, John L. *SOG: The Secret Wars of America's Commandos in Vietnam.* New York: Onyx Books, 1998.

Popovic, Milos. "Fragile Proxies: Explaining Rebel Defection against Their State Sponsors." *Terrorism and Political Violence* 29, no. 5 (2017): 922–942.

Powers, Rod. "Law of Armed Conflict (LOAC)—The Rules of War." The Balance Careers. October 27, 2016. https://www.thebalancecareers.com/law-of-armed-conflict-loac-3332966.

PRI. "A Timeline of the Islamic State's Gains and Losses in Iraq and Syria." February 19, 2017. https://www.pri.org/stories/2017-02-19/timeline-islamic-states-gains-and-losses-iraq-and-syria.

Priest, Dana. "An Unconventional Soldier." *Washington Post,* December 23, 2001. https://www.washingtonpost.com/archive/politics/2001/12/23/an-unconventional-soldier/1ed14185-3b2c-4165-9d7f-5f4d9cc878c4/.

Pruitt, Sarah. "Navy SEALs: 10 Key Missions." History. January 5, 2017. http://www.history.com/news/navy-seals-10-key-missions.

Rao, Jay. "W. L. Gore: Culture of Innovation." Babson College case BAB698. Babson Park, MA: Babson College, 2012.

Rasmussen, Anders Fogh. "Security Policy in an Era of Budgetary Constraint." North Atlantic Treaty Organization. June 21, 2010. https://www.nato.int/cps/en/natolive/opinions_64563.htm.

Record, Jeffrey. "Why the Strong Lose." *Parameters* 35, no. 4 (2005): 16–31.

Reeder Jr., Edward M. "Our Only Security Is Our Ability to Change." *Special Warfare* 26, no. 4 (October 2013): 4.

Resolute Support Afghanistan. "NATO Resolute Support History." Accessed September 15, 2018. https://rs.nato.int/about-us/history/isaf-history.aspx.

Robinson, Linda. "The Future of Special Operations: Beyond Kill and Capture." *Foreign Affairs* 91, no. 6 (2012): 110–122. http://www.jstor.org.libproxy.nps.edu/stable/41720938.

Robinson, Linda, Austin Long, Kimberly Jackson, and Rebeca Orrie. *Improving the Understanding of Special Operations: A Case History Analysis.* Santa Monica, CA: RAND Corporation, 2018. https://doi.org/10.7249/RR2026.

Roggio, Billy, and Lisa Lundquist, "Green-on-Blue Attacks in Afghanistan: The Data." *Long War Journal.* Last modified June 17, 2017. http://www.longwarjournal. org/archives/2012/08/green-on-blue_attack.php.

Rothstein, Hy S. "A Tale of Two Wars: Why the U.S. Cannot Conduct Unconventional Warfare." PhD diss., Tufts University, MA: 2004.

———. *Afghanistan and the Troubled Future of Unconventional Warfare.* Annapolis, MD: Naval Institute Press, 2006.

Salehyan, Idean. "The Delegation of War to Rebel Organizations." *The Journal of Conflict Resolution* 54, no. 3 (June 2010): 493–515.

Salehyan, Idean, David Siroky, and Reed M. Wood. "External Rebel Sponsorship and Civilian Abuse: A Principal-Agent Analysis of Wartime Atrocities." *International Organization* 68, no. 3 (2014): 633–661.

Sandomir, Richard. "Recalling the Terror in Munich." *New York Times,* September 2, 2002. https://www.nytimes.com/2002/09/02/sports/tv-sports-recalling-the-terror-in-munich.html.

Schaub, Gary. "Denmark: Defense Woes in the Little U.S. Ally That Could." War on the Rocks. August 6, 2015. https://warontherocks.com/2015/08/denmark-defense-woes-in-the-little-u-s-ally-that-could/.

Schröer, Arne. "Lessons Learned? German Security Policy and the War in Afghanistan." *German Politics* 23, no. 1–2 (2014): 1–25. https://doi.org/10.1080/09644008.2014.916691.

Schuurman, Paul. "War as a System: A Three-Stage Model for the Development of Clausewitz's Thinking on Military Conflict and Its Constraints." *Journal of Strategic Studies* 37, no. 6–7

(2014): 926–948. https://doi.org/10.1080/
01402390.2014.933316.

Seaman, Andrew M. "U.S. Military 'Golden Hour' Rule Saved Lives."
Reuters. September 30, 2015. https://www.reuters.com/
article/us-health-trauma-transport/u-s-military-golden-hour-
rule-saved-lives-idUSKCN0RU31F20150930.

SIGAR. "Reconstructing-the-ANDSF." September 2017.
https://www.sigar.mil/interactive-reports/reconstructing-the-
andsf/index.html.

Simons, Anna. *Got Vision? Unity of Vision in Policy and Strategy: What It
Is, and Why We Need It.* Carlisle, PA: Strategic Studies Institute,
2010.

Sjoholm, John. "Denmark Deploys Army Special Forces to Syria."
Lima Charlie News, January 22, 2017.
https://limacharlienews.com/mena/denmark-deploys-army-
special-forces-to-syria/.

Sof, Eric. "Denmark SOF: Jaegerkorpset and Froemandskorpset."
[Denmark SOF: Danish Army SOF and Danish Navy SEALs]
Special Ops Magazine (blog), May 14, 2013. https://special-
ops.org/sof/unit/denmark-sof-jaegerkorpset-and-
froemandskorpset/.

Special Operations Command. *Special Operations,* JP 3–05. Washington, DC: Department of Defense, 2011. http://www.jcs.mil/
Portals/36/Documents/Doctrine/pubs/jp3_05.pdf.

Starr, Barbara, and Jamie Crawford. "Exclusive: Inside the Rarely-
Acknowledged Missions of Two Navy SEALs Killed in Action." CNN. June 12, 2017. https://www.cnn.com/2017/06/
12/politics/us-navy-seals-ryan-owens-kyle-milliken/
index.html.

Stolzoff, Sam G. *The Iraqi Tribal System: A Reference for Social Scientists,
Analysts, and Tribal Engagement.* Minneapolis, MN: Two Harbors Press, 2009.

Sullivan, Patricia. *Who Wins?: Predicting Strategic Success and Failure in
Armed Conflict.* New York: Oxford University Press, 2012.

Sünkler, Sören. *Die Spezialverbände der Bundeswehr.* [The Special Units of the German armed forces] Stuttgart: Motorbuch, 2007.

———. *Elite- und Spezialeinheiten Europas.* [Elite and Special Units of Europe] Stuttgart: Motorbuch, 2008.

Taylor, Adam. "Why It Matters That U.S. Troops Are in Iraq's Troubled Anbar Province—Again." *Washington Post,* November 12, 2014. https://www. washingtonpost.com/news/worldviews/wp/2014/11/12/why-it-matters-that-u-s-troops-are-in-iraqs-troubled-anbar-province-again/.

Thornton, Rob. "BPC and the Indirect vs. Direct Approach in the Long War." *Small Wars Journal* (blog), accessed May 22, 2018. http://smallwarsjournal.com/blog/bpc-and-the-indirect-vs-direct-approach-in-the-long-war.

Tovo, Kenneth E. *USASOC Strategy-2035.* Tampa, FL: United States Army Special Operations Command, April 2016. http://www.soc.mil/AssortedPages/USASOCStrategy2035.pdf.

Tucker, David, and Christopher Lamb. *Restructuring Special Operations Forces for Emerging Threats.* Washington, DC: Institute for National Strategic Studies, 2006.

———. *United States Special Operations Forces.* New York: Columbia University Press, 2007.

Tucker, Spencer, and Paul G. Pierpaoli. *U.S. Conflicts in the 21st Century: Afghanistan War, Iraq War, and the War on Terror.* Santa Barbara, CA: ABC-CLIO, 2016.

Tugwell, Maurice, and David Charter. "Special Operations and the Threats to United States Interest in the 1980s." In *Special Operations in U.S. Strategy,* edited by Frank R. Barnett, B. Hugh Tovar, and Richard H. Schultz. Washington, DC: National Defense University Press, 1984.

Turse, Nick. "American Special Ops Forces Have Deployed to 70 Percent of the World's Countries in 2017." *The Nation,* June 26, 2017. https://www.thenation.com/article/american-special-ops-forces-have-deployed-to-70-percent-of-the-worlds-countries-in-2017/.

Vandenbroucke, Lucien S. *Perilous Options: Special Operations as an Instrument of U.S. Foreign Policy.* New York: Oxford University Press, 1993.

Votel, Joseph L. "The Posture of U.S. Central Command." United States Central Command. March 9, 2017. https://www.centcom.mil/Portals/6/Documents/Votel_03–09-17.pdf.

Votel, Joseph L., Charles T. Cleveland, Charles T. Connett, and Will Irwin. "Unconventional Warfare in the Gray Zone." *Joint Force Quarterly* 80, no. 1 (January 2016): 101–109.

Warrick, Joby. *Black Flags: The Rise of ISIS.* New York: Anchor Books, 2016.

Weiss, Jim, and Mickey Davis. "Bundespolizei: Germany's Federal Police." *Law & Order* 58, no. 7 (2010): 46–49.

Werner, Lars. "Adaptive Reorganization of German Special Operations Forces." Master's thesis, Naval Postgraduate School, 2013. http://hdl.handle.net/10945/39035.

Whiteside, Craig. "War, Interrupted, Part I: The Roots of the Jihadist Resurgence in Iraq." War on the Rocks. November 2014. https://warontherocks.com/2014/11/war-interrupted-part-i-the-roots-of-the-jihadist-resurgence-in-iraq/.

Williams, Brian Glyn. "Fighting with a Double-Edged Sword: Proxy Militias in Iraq, Afghanistan, Bosnia, and Chechnya." In *Making Sense of Proxy Wars: States, Surrogates & the Use of Force,* edited by William Banks, 61–88. Lincoln NE: Potomac Books, 2012.

Williams, David. "Ousting ISIS from Al Anbar: The Advise and Assist Mission of Task Force Al Asad." Marines. July 31, 2017. https://www.marines.mil/News/News-Display/Article/1262206/ousting-isis-from-al-anbar-the-advise-and-assist-mission-of-task-force-al-asad/.

Carola Hartmann Miles-Verlag

<u>Militär und Gesellschaft</u>

Eberhard Birk, Winfried Heinemann, Sven Lange (Hrsg.), *Tradition für die Bundeswehr. Neue Aspekte einer alten Debatte,* Berlin 2012.

Angelika Dörfler-Dierken, *Führung in der Bundeswehr,* Berlin 2013.

Wolf Graf von Baudissin, *Grundwert Frieden in Politik – Strategie – Führung von Streitkräften,* hrsg. von Claus von Rosen, Berlin 2014.

Marcel Bohnert, Lukas J. Reitstetter (Hrsg.), *Armee im Aufbruch. Zur Gedankenwelt junger Offiziere in den Kampftruppen der Bundeswehr,* Berlin 2014.

Arjan Kozica, Kai Prüter, Hannes Wendroth (Hrsg.), *Unternehmen Bundeswehr? Theorie und Praxis (militärischer) Führung,* Berlin 2014.

Angelika Dörfler-Dierken, Robert Kramer, *Innere Führung in Zahlen. Streitkräftebefragung 2013,* Berlin 2014.

Phil C. Langer, Gerhard Kümmel (Hrsg.), *„Wir sind Bundeswehr." Wie viel Vielfalt benötigen/vertragen die Streitkräfte?,* Berlin 2015.

Alois Bach, Walter Sauer (Hrsg.), *Schützen.Retten.Kämpfen. Dienen für Deutschland,* Berlin 2016.

Marcel Bohnert, Björn Schreiber (Hrsg.), *Die unsichtbaren Veteranen. Kriegsheimkehrer in der deutschen Gesellschaft,* Berlin 2016.

Donald Abenheim and Carolyn Halladay, *Soldiers, War, Knowledge and Citizenship: German-American Essays on Civil-Military Relations,* Berlin 2017.

Dirk Freudenberg, *Theorie des Irregulären. Erscheinungen und Abgrenzungen von Partisanen, Guerillas und Terroristen im Modernen Kleinkrieg sowie Entwicklungstendenzen der Reaktion, 3 Bde.,* Berlin 2018.

Markus Reisner, *Robotic Wars – Legitimatorische Grundlagen und Grenzen des Einsatzes von Military Unmanned Systems in modernen Konfliktszenarien,* Berlin 2018.

Angelika Dörfler-Dierken (Hrsg.), *Hinschauen! Geschlecht, Rechtspopulismus, Rituale: Systemische Probleme oder individuelles Fehlverhalten?,* Berlin 2019.

Erinnerungen und Tradition

Blue Braun, *Erinnerungen an die Marine 1956–1996,* Berlin 2012.

Harald Volkmar Schlieder, *Kommando zurück!,* Berlin 2012.

Klaus Grot, *So war's, damals. Dienstchronik eines Pionieroffiziers im Kalten Krieg 1954–1991,* Berlin 2014.

Gustav Lünenborg, *Bürger und Soldat. Innere Führung hautnah 1956– 1993, 1993–2015,* Berlin 2015.

Adolf Brüggemann, *Als Offizier der Bundeswehr im Auswärtigen Dienst. Meine Erinnerungen als Militärattaché in Seoul (Republik Korea) 1978–83 und in Prag (Tschechoslowakei/Tschechien) 1988–1993,* Berlin 2015.

Rainer Buske, *Eine Reise ins Innere der Bundeswehr. Wundersame Geschichten aus einer anderen Welt,* Berlin 2016.

Heinz Laube, *Duell am Himmel,* Berlin 2016.

Viktor Toyka, *Dienst in Zeiten des Wandels. Erinnerungen aus 40 Jahren Dienst als Marineoffizier 1966-2000,* Berlin 2017.

Dieter Hanel, *Military Link. Sicherheitspolitische Zeitreise eines Offiziers und Rüstungsmanagers,* Berlin 2018.

Joachim Welz, *Vom Kontingentsheer zum Reichsheer: Militärkonventionen als Motor der Wehrverfassung,* Berlin 2018.

Donald Abenheim, Uwe Hartmann (Hrsg.), *Tradition in der Bundeswehr. Zum Erbe des deutschen Soldaten und zur Umsetzung des neuen Traditionserlasses,* Berlin 2018.

Standpunkte und Orientierungen

Daniel Giese, *Militärische Führung im Internetzeitalter – Die Bedeutung von Strategischer Kommunikation und Social Media für Entscheidungsprozesse, Organisationsstrukturen und Führerausbildung in der Bundeswehr,* Berlin 2014.

Dirk Freudenberg, *Auftragstaktik und Innere Führung. Feststellungen und Anmerkungen zur Frage nach Bedeutung und Verhältnis des inneren Gefüges und der Auftragstaktik unter den Bedingungen des Einsatzes der Deutschen Bundeswehr,* Berlin 2014.

Uwe Hartmann (Hrsg.), *Lernen von Afghanistan. Innovative Mittel und Wege für Auslandseinsätze,* Berlin 2015.

Fouzieh Melanie Alamir, *Vernetzte Sicherheit – Quo Vadis?*, Berlin 2015.

Hartwig von Schubert, *Integrative Militärethik. Ethische Urteilsbildung in der militärischen Führung*, Berlin 2015.

Uwe Hartmann, *Hybrider Krieg als neue Bedrohung von Freiheit und Frieden. Zur Relevanz der Inneren Führung in Politik, Gesellschaft und Streitkräften*, Berlin 2015.

Klaus Beckmann, *Treue.Bürgermut.Ungehorsam. Anstöße zur Führungskultur und zum beruflichen Selbstverständnis in der Bundeswehr*, Berlin 2015.

Florian Beerenkämper, Marcel Bohnert, Anja Buresch, Sandra Matuszewski, *Der innerafghanische Friedens- und Aussöhnungsprozess*, Berlin 2016.

Martin Sebaldt, *Nicht abwehrbereit. Die Kardinalprobleme der deutschen Streitkräfte, der Offenbarungseid des Weißbuchs und die Wege aus der Gefahr*, Berlin 2017.

Christian J. Grothaus, *Der „hybride Krieg" vor dem Hintergrund der kollektiven Gedächtnisse Estlands, Lettlands und Litauens*, Berlin 2017.

Uwe Hartmann, *Der gute Soldat. Politische Kultur und soldatisches Selbstverständnis heute*, Berlin 2018.

Christian Bauer, Marcel Bohnert, Jan Pahl, *Vitalis Innere Führung! Zum Status Quo der Führungskultur in den deutschen Streitkräften*, Berlin 2018.

Militärgeschichte

Eberhard Kliem, Kathrin Orth, *"Wir wurden wie blödsinnig vom Feind beschossen". Menschen und Schiffe in der Skagerrakschlacht 1916*, Berlin 2016.

Eberhard Birk, *"Auf Euch ruht das Heil meines theuern Württemberg!". Das Gefecht bei Tauberbischofsheim am 24. Juli 1866 im Spiegel der württembergischen Heeresgeschichte des 19. Jahrhunderts*, Berlin 2016.

Eckhard Lisec, *Der Unabhängigkeitskrieg und die Gründung der Türkei 1919–1923*, Berlin 2016.

Hans Frank, Norbert Rath, *Kommodore Rudolf Petersen. Führer der Schnellboote 1942–1945. Ein Leben in Licht und Schatten unteilbarer Verantwortung*, Berlin 2016.

117

Eckhard Lisec, *Der Völkermord an den Armeniern im 1. Weltkrieg – Deutsche Offiziere beteiligt?,* Berlin 2017.

Ingo Pfeiffer, *Heinz Neukirchen. Marinekarriere an wechselnden Fronten,* Berlin 2017.

Siegfried Lautsch, *Grundzüge des operativen Denkens in der NATO. Ein zeitgeschichtlicher Rückblick auf die 1980er Jahre,* Berlin ²2018.

Eckhard Lisec, *Die Türkische Armee – Von Mete Han (209 v. Chr.) über Atatürk zur Gegenwart,* Berlin 2018.

Joachim Welz, *Erfolgsstory oder Trauma – die Übernahme von Armeen. Lehren aus der Übernahme des österreichischen Bundesheeres in die Wehrmacht 1938 und der Reste der NVA in die Bundeswehr 1990,* Berlin 2018.

Joachim Welz, *Vom Kontingentsheer zum Reichsheer. Militärkonventionen als Motor der Wehrverfassung,* Berlin 2018.

Georg Neuhaus, *Am Anfang war ein Speer. Eine Chronographie der Kriegs- und Militärtechnologien,* Berlin 2018.

Hans Delbrück / Peter Paret, *Krieg, Geschichte, Theorie. Zwei Studien über Clausewitz, herausgegeben von Peter Paret,* Berlin 2018.

Einsatzerfahrungen

Kay Kuhlen, *Um des lieben Friedens willen. Als Peacekeeper im Kosovo,* Eschede 2009.

Sascha Brinkmann, Joachim Hoppe (Hrsg.), *Generation Einsatz, Fallschirmjäger berichten ihre Erfahrungen aus Afghanistan,* Berlin 2010.

Artur Schwitalla, *Afghanistan, jetzt weiß ich erst... Gedanken aus meiner Zeit als Kommandeur des Provincial Reconstruction Team FEYZABAD,* Berlin 2010.

Uwe Hartmann, *War without Fighting? The Reintegration of Former Combatants in Afghanistan seen through the Lens of Strategic Thought,* Berlin 2014.

Rainer Buske, *KUNDUZ. Ein Erlebnisbericht über einen militärischen Einsatz der Bundeswehr in AFGHANISTAN im Jahre 2008,* Berlin ²2016.

Marcel Bohnert, Andy Neumann, *German Mechanized Infantry on Combat Operations in Afghanistan,* Berlin 2017.

Monterey Studies

Uwe Hartmann, *Carl von Clausewitz and the Making of Modern Strategy,* Potsdam 2002.

Zeljko Cepanec, *Croatia and NATO. The Stony Road to Membership,* Potsdam 2002.

Ekkehard Stemmer, *Demography and European Armed Forces,* Berlin 2006.

Sven Lange, *Revolt against the West. A Comparison of the Current War on Terror with the Boxer Rebellion in 1900-01,* Berlin 2007.

Klaus M. Brust, *Culture and the Transformation of the Bundeswehr,* Berlin 2007.

Donald Abenheim, *Soldier and Politics Transformed,* Berlin 2007.

Michael Stolzke, *The Conflict Aftermath. A Chance for Democracy: Norm Diffusion in Post-Conflict Peace Building,* Berlin 2007.

Frank Reimers, *Security Culture in Times of War. How did the Balkan War affect the Security Cultures in Germany and the United States?,* Berlin 2007.

Michael G. Lux, *Innere Führung – A Superior Concept of Leadership?,* Berlin 2009.

Marc A. Walther, *HAMAS between Violence and Pragmatism,* Berlin 2010.

Frank Hagemann, *Strategy Making in the European Union,* Berlin 2010.

Ralf Hammerstein, *Deliberalization in Jordan: the Roles of Islamists and U.S.-EU Assistance in stalled Democratization,* Berlin 2011.

Jochen Wittmann, *Auftragstaktik,* Berlin 2012.

Michael Hanisch, *On German Foreign und Security Policy. Determinants of German Military Engagement in Africa since 2011,* Berlin 2015.

Grégoire Monnet, *The Evolution of Strategic Thought Since September 11, 2001,* Berlin 2016.

Stefan Klein, *America First? Isolationism in U.S. Foreign Policy from the 19th to the 21st Century,* Berlin 2017.

Jahrbuch Innere Führung

Uwe Hartmann, Claus von Rosen, Christian Walther (Hrsg.), *Jahrbuch Innere Führung 2009. Die Rückkehr des Soldatischen,* Eschede 2009.

Helmut R. Hammerich, Uwe Hartmann, Claus von Rosen (Hrsg.), *Jahrbuch Innere Führung 2010. Die Grenzen des Militärischen,* Berlin 2010.

Uwe Hartmann, Claus von Rosen, Christian Walther (Hrsg.), *Jahrbuch Innere Führung 2011. Ethik als geistige Rüstung für Soldaten,* Berlin 2011.

Uwe Hartmann, Claus von Rosen, Christian Walther (Hrsg.), *Jahrbuch Innere Führung 2012. Der Soldatenberuf zwischen gesellschaftlicher Integration und suis generis-Ansprüchen,* Berlin 2012.

Uwe Hartmann, Claus von Rosen (Hrsg.), *Jahrbuch Innere Führung 2013. Wissenschaften und ihre Relevanz für die Bundeswehr als Armee im Einsatz,* Berlin 2013.

Uwe Hartmann, Claus von Rosen (Hrsg.), *Jahrbuch Innere Führung 2014. Drohnen, Roboter und Cyborgs – Der Soldat im Angesicht neuer Militärtechnologien,* Berlin 2014.

Uwe Hartmann, Claus von Rosen (Hrsg.), *Jahrbuch Innere Führung 2015. Neue Denkwege angesichts der Gleichzeitigkeit unterschiedlicher Krisen, Konflikte und Kriege,* Berlin 2015.

Uwe Hartmann, Claus von Rosen (Hrsg.), *Jahrbuch Innere Führung 2016. Innere Führung als kritische Instanz,* Berlin 2016.

Uwe Hartmann, Claus von Rosen (Hrsg.), *Jahrbuch Innere Führung 2017. Die Wiederkehr der Verteidigung in Europa und die Zukunft der Bundeswehr,* Berlin 2017.

Uwe Hartmann, Claus von Rosen (Hrsg.), *Jahrbuch Innere Führung 2018. Innere Führung zwischen Aufbruch, Abbau und Sbschaffung: Neues denken, Mitgestaltung fördern, Alternativen wagen,* Berlin 2018.

www.miles-verlag.jimdo.com